The Zoni English System 4

WRITING TEAM: Millie Agostino
     Wilmer Guerrero

METHODOLOGY TEAM: Pat Ossa
     Zoilo C. Nieto
     Keith W. Hansen, Ph.D.

EDITOR: Keith W. Hansen, Ph.D.

DIRECTOR: Zoilo C. Nieto

D1127746

ZONI™
E N G L I S H
S Y S T E M
A Unique Classroom Instructional Method™

Foreword

The *Zoni English System* has been designed as a classroom instructional method in response to the demonstrated great needs of nonnative speakers of English in everyday life in English-speaking countries.

Since communication is essential for survival, the *Zoni English System* method is based on daily life situations while explaining fundamental expressions as well as grammatical structures. In so doing, we have also employed a high-frequency vocabulary. An effective textual material increases the student's motivation to continue studying English by influencing his or her attitude toward learning as well as enhancing his or her future possibilities.

Objectives

The *Zoni English System* achieves these objectives:
1. To reach out to accommodate students of diverse backgrounds
2. To create a universal program for anyone who wants to learn practical English
3. To make students think in English
4. To encourage students to lose any fear of the language
5. To keep student motivation high in the learning process
6. To build up students' fluency

The *Zoni English System 4 second edition* features 5 graphic-rich, student-centered-learning lessons that build on the previous *Zoni English System* topics and introduce new, high-usage material such as comparatives, modal verbs, fundamental prepositions and the present perfect and present perfect progressive tenses. A variety of creative, proven techniques are utilized to facilitate the achievement of the *Zoni English System* objectives.

TO THE TEACHER

<u>In the classroom</u>
Teacher talking time 25%
Student talking time 75%

Techniques to be employed:

Instructors utilize such teaching techniques as:
- C.I.P.: Choral Intonation Practice
- Backward build-up (expansion) drill
- Elicitation
- Vanishing
- Interaction
- Role playing
- Using commands to direct behavior
- Action sequence
- Getting students to practice self-correction
- Conversation practice
- Single-slot substitution drills
- Multiple-slot substitution drills
- Chain drills
- Transformation drills
- Teacher's silence
- Word charts
- Structured feedback
- Positive suggestion
- Question and answer exercises
- Language games: information gap, choice, feedback, party time
  (See the Zoni Teacher's Manual.)
- Fill-in-the-blank exercises
- Peripheral learning
- Dictation (find scripts in the Zoni Teacher's Manual.)

<u>Lesson plan/technique explanations are available for instructors.</u>

For teachers that have not gone through the Zoni co-teaching program, the methodology and techniques detailed in the **Zoni Teacher's Manual** must be followed.

Important symbols: **They are found throughout the book.**

When you see these symbols, use the substitution drill. This will encourage students to enrich their vocabulary by using various nouns, adjectives, verbs, etc.

Teachers have to continue eliciting to complete the interaction with the entire class participating.

Teachers have to make groups of 2 students for the Pair Practice period.

Teachers ask students to stand up and perform their dialogues.

Zoni English System 4 continues the emphasis on group work in the classroom and takes it further by increasing the student-centered nature of the classroom. This is achieved through the introduction of Group Oral Interaction pages and exercises where groups of three students ("triangulation") work together on previously introduced material in a real communicative fashion. This increased weight given to student-centered learning in the Zoni classroom facilitates the enhanced, simultaneous usage of all four language skills by each and every student during greater amounts of class time, thereby maximizing student learning and progress in the classroom. (See the Zoni Teacher's Manual for more discussion of the Group Oral Interaction process.)

CLASSROOM SEATING ARRANGEMENTS

In addition to teachers' varying their teaching routines, we also encourage teachers to vary their classroom seating arrangements based on what is being taught. The seating arrangements will depend upon the number of students and classroom size.

Standard

This type of seating arrangement, where students are arranged in rows, is generally used for lecture-type lessons and presentations. It is also beneficial when we need all the students to be focused on a particular task on the board. Students are able to work at their own pace doing their work. It tends to be teacher-centered. The teacher must circulate and have lots of eye contact with his/her students to make sure all are involved.

In the Zoni System, we generally begin with this seating arrangement when introducing a grammar point.

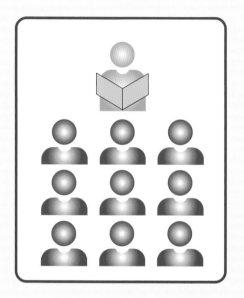

Semi-circle

This seating arrangement is recommended when we want to have maximum student interaction while focused on a particular task such as getting information from the board, watching a video or listening to a tape. Students are able to see their classmates' body and facial expressions easily during the discussions. It is less teacher-centered, so there is a lot of student interaction.

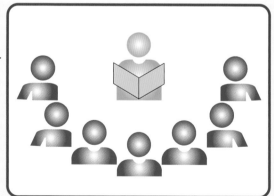

Circle: group work

Group work generally consists of three or more students. There is maximum student participation. Students are more relaxed about experimenting with the language, and the fear of making a mistake is diminished. Group work is a cooperative learning experience where students not only learn from their teacher but also from their classmates.

Pair work

The same conditions exist as with group work but with 2 students.

In the lower levels, the Zoni System incorporates a lot of group work and/or pair work during the Practice Period sessions.

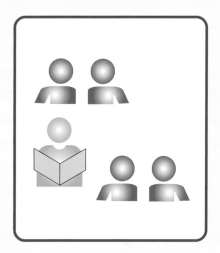

Homework

When we assign homework to students, it is important that we also check it in the following class. Checking homework should not take more than 15 minutes. Make sure you check all students' homework. Vary your checking homework routine; for example, check it in the second hour of class. Finally, keep a record of which students have not done their homework. For each assignment not completed, a student gets a zero. Warn the student that should s/he get a lot of homework zeroes, s/he may have to repeat the course.

SURPRISE FACTOR

Though developing a routine in the classroom is good, at other times, it is critical that teachers change their classroom routines to keep students on their toes.

Some examples in using the surprise factor are:

1. Checking the homework in the second hour of the class period instead of at the beginning of the class period.
2. Asking the class a question, then zeroing in and calling on a student to answer it.

INDISPENSABLE ORAL PRACTICE

The command "listen and repeat" is found throughout the book. This technique consists of the presentation of semantic illustrations and graphics that the instructor demonstrates and to which the students respond. In addition to the use of question and answer sessions, the *Zoni English System* encourages choral and individual repetition in order to improve the student's pronunciation and to lose any fear of the language. Teachers should not be reluctant to practice pronunciation even with upper-level students; all students of any level benefit from this frequent practice. Teachers should also ensure that students are not taking notes or otherwise writing during all oral practice. The focus must remain on the oral exercise.

ELICIT FROM THE STUDENTS

Elicit all vocabulary and examples from the students. Take advantage of students' prior knowledge. By doing so, we share their knowledge with the rest of the class, build confidence, promote active thinking and stimulate students to come up with interesting examples in the dialogues.

BOARD WORK

At Zoni, we believe in keeping the board work as simple as possible, especially when teaching the beginner and intermediate levels. Board work is beneficial in that teachers can use it as a resource for student practice when doing Choral Intonation Practice (CIP), drilling and role playing. Board work keeps students focused. Board work reinforces reading and spelling.

While doing board work, make sure *all* students have their books and notebooks *closed. No* writing or copying is allowed during this period. All students must be focused on the board. Write in print, not script. Plan ahead what you will be putting on the board. If writing a long dialogue, work your dialogue one segment at a time. We strongly recommend that teachers follow our board work examples seen in the Zoni Teacher's Manual.

ATTENDANCE

Learning English is a matter of constant, consistent practice and dedication. Student attendance is vital for maximum learning and benefits; this is why teachers must remind students that regular attendance is necessary. If students do not comply, they may be asked to take the course again. Attendance should not be taken for granted. Encouragement and reminders about class attendance are essential.

ACKNOWLEDGMENTS

I'm very happy and proud to see the publication of a new chapter of the *Zoni English System* series: *Zoni English System 4*. A large number of people have been involved in this project; it is due to their passion, persistent dedication and cooperation that the *Zoni English System 4* has been completed. I would like to give special thanks to **Masami Soeda** for her continued, outstanding graphic-design work. In particular, I want to thank **Cristina Cotto** and **Hakan Mansuroglu** for their valuable input. I would also like to thank the Zoni faculty for their cooperation and suggestions. And I want to recognize the contributions from Zoni Language Centers students who have provided us with much-needed feedback.

Zoilo C. Nieto
Director

TABLE OF CONTENTS

ZONI ENGLISH SYSTEM ©

Dear Zoni Student,

We would like to welcome you to our *Zoni English System 4*. We would also like to remind you that, in order to get the most out of your English study, you should always do the following:

-Speak only English in class
-Attend class every day
-Do all assigned homework

Relax and have fun!

Lesson 1

COMPARATIVE

SUPERLATIVE

COMPARATIVE

SUPERLATIVE

See Teacher's Manual

(Listen and repeat)

Example

> **Which city has more people: New York or Paris?**
>
> New York has **more people than** Paris.
>
> Paris has **fewer people than** New York.

> **Which city has more traffic: London or Paris?**
>
> _____ has **more traffic than** _____.

Which city has...?

New York   Paris

ZONI ENGLISH SYSTEM ©

Which city has less traffic: Tokyo or Paris?

_____ has **less traffic than** _____.

Which city has the most people?

_____ has **the most people**.

Which city has the least traffic?

_____ has **the least traffic**.

Oral Practice

(Elicit from the students)

1. London _____

2. Tokyo _____

3. _____

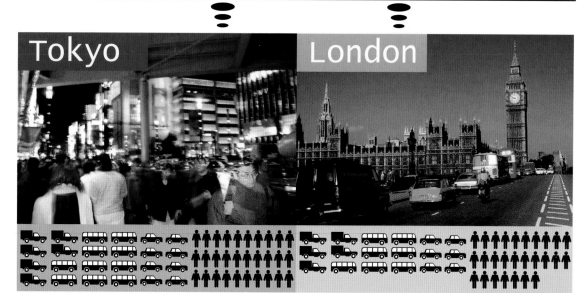

Comparative

Nouns = Names

*Count nouns name people, places and things that you can count.

*Noncount nouns name things that you cannot count.

Count Nouns (1, 2, 3,...)	Noncount Nouns (= 1 mass)
dollars	money

days	time

batteries attractions songs wars bagels	energy entertainment music peace bread
_____	_____
_____	_____

 Peter   Eric

(Listen and repeat)

Comparative ⟶

more *noun* than

Count Nouns

Who has more *dollars*: Eric or Peter?

Eric has more *dollars* than Peter.

Noncount Nouns

Who has more *money*: Eric or Peter?

Eric has more *money* than Peter.

Comparative ⟶

fewer *noun* than

Count Nouns

Who has fewer *dollars*: Eric or Peter?

Peter has fewer *dollars* than Eric.

less *noun* than

Noncount Nouns

Who has less *money*: Eric or Peter?

Peter has less *money* than Eric.

Group Oral Interaction

In groups, see the sample pictures on page 7 and complete the following dialogue.

see the sample pictures on page 7

Example: **Comparative** ⟶ (+)

days

Who has more **days** to study for the final exam: Cindy or Linda?

Cindy has more **days** to study than Linda.

---

time

Who has more **time** to study for the final exam: Cindy or Linda?

Cindy has more **time** to study than Linda.

---

1. *bottles*

Who _____

_____

---

water

Who _____

_____

---

2. *students*

Which classroom _____

_____

energy

Which classroom _____

_____

3. *cars*

Which city _____

_____

pollution

Which city _____

_____

4. *facts*

Which source _____

_____

information

Which source _____

_____

I'm going to take the final exam **tomorrow**. I have to study tonight.

Linda

My exam is **next week**. I still have time to study.

Cindy

Example

Jennifer

Mike

1.

Class A

Class B

2.

City A

City B

3.

an encyclopedia

a magazine

4.

Group Oral Interaction

In groups, see the sample pictures on page 7 and complete the following dialogue.

see the sample pictures on page 7

Example: **Comparative** ⟶ ⊖

days

Who has *fewer* **days** to study for the final exam: Cindy or Linda?

Linda has *fewer* **days** to study than Cindy.

- -

time

Who has *less* **time** to study for the final exam: Cindy or Linda?

Linda has *less* **time** to study than Cindy.

1. *bottles*

   Who _____

   _____

- -

   water

   Who _____

   _____

2. *students*

   Which classroom _____

   _____

ZONI ENGLISH SYSTEM ©

energy

Which classroom _____

_____

3. *cars*

Which city _____

_____

pollution

Which city _____

_____

4. *facts*

Which source _____

_____

information

Which source _____

_____

Group Oral Interaction

In groups, make a comparison based on the pictures and information below. *(Teachers: Assess the Comparative here.)*

See Teacher's Manual

Example:

a gold ring

a silver ring

A gold ring costs more money than a silver ring.

(costs / money)

1

river

ocean

A river _____.

(has / water)

2

green bowl   yellow bowl

The green bowl _____.

(contains / rice)

3

a car

a motorcycle

A motorcycle _____.

(holds / people)

4

a grandfather   a granddaughter

A grandfather _____.

(has / experience)

5

a bank

a wallet

A wallet usually_____.

(has / money)

ZONI ENGLISH SYSTEM ©

Homework

Change the following comparative adjectives to comparative nouns.

Example: Mary is friendlier than Anita. **(friends)**

Mary has <u>more friends than Anita.</u>

1. Arthur is not as wealthy as his father. **(money)**

   Arthur has _____

2. Canada is colder than the U.S. **(snow)**

   Canada receives _____

3. Lisa is not as busy as Miguel. **(work)**

   Lisa has_____

4. Genoa is not as popular as Rome. **(tourists)**

   Genoa has_____

5. Ivan is more careless than Andres. **(mistakes)**

   Ivan makes _____

6. My apartment building is newer than yours. **(repairs)**

   My apartment building needs _____

7. My brother is busier than my sister. **(free time)**

   My brother has _____

Superlative

Peter   Eric   Carla

(Listen and repeat)

Superlative ⟶ ⊕

The most *noun*

Count Nouns

Who has <u>the most</u> *dollars*: Eric, Peter or Carla?

Carla has <u>the most</u> *dollars* of the three.

Noncount Nouns

Who has <u>the most</u> *money*: Eric, Peter or Carla?

Carla has <u>the most</u> *money* of the three.

Superlative ⟶ ⊖

The fewest *noun*

Count Nouns

Who has <u>the fewest</u> *dollars*: Eric, Peter or Carla?

Peter has <u>the fewest</u> *dollars* of the three.

The least *noun*

Noncount Nouns

Who has <u>the least</u> *money*: Eric, Peter or Carla?

Peter has <u>the least</u> *money* of the three.

Group Oral Interaction

In groups, see the sample pictures on page 15 and complete the following dialogue.

Example:

Superlative ⟶ ➕

days

Who has the most **days** to study for the final exam?

Chris has the most **days** to study.

time

Who has the most **time** to study for the final exam?

Chris has the most **time** to study.

1. *bottles*

Who _____

_____

water

Who _____

_____

2. *students*

Which classroom _____

_____

energy

Which classroom _____

_____

3. *cars*

Which city _____

_____

pollution

Which city _____

_____

4. *facts*

Which source _____

_____

information

Which source _____

_____

14

Example

Chris: I'm going to take the final exam **in 2 weeks**.

Linda: I'm going to take the final exam **tomorrow**.

Cindy: My exam is **next week**.

1.

Jennifer

Mike

Donna

2.

Class A

Class B

Class C

3.

City A

City B

City C

4.

a comic book

an encyclopedia

a magazine

Group Oral Interaction

In groups, see the sample pictures on page 15 and complete the following dialogue.

Example:

Superlative ⟶ —

days

Who has the fewest **days** to study for the final exam?

Linda has the fewest **days** to study.

---

time

Who has the least **time** to study for the final exam?

Linda has the least **time** to study.

1. *bottles*

Who _____

_____

---

water

Who _____

_____

2. *students*

Which classroom _____

_____

energy

Which classroom _____

_____

3. *cars*

Which city _____

_____

pollution

Which city _____

_____

4. *facts*

Which source _____

_____

information

Which source _____

_____

Group Oral Interaction

In groups, answer the following questions using <u>most</u>, <u>least</u> or <u>fewest</u>.

1. Which part of a summer's day has

a. the _____ sunlight +

b. the _____ sunlight -

?

| 1:00 PM | 6:30 PM | 8:30 PM |

2. Which food contains

a. the _____ calories +

b. the _____ calories -

?

470 calories

80 calories

350 calories

sushi

a small salad

a cheeseburger

3. On Mondays, at what time of the day do you usually see

a. the _____ cars +

b. the _____ cars -

?

12:00 AM midnight	1:30 PM	9:00 AM

4. In New York, what month usually has

a. the _____ beachgoers +

b. the _____ beachgoers -

?

April	July	February

5. Which type of milk contains

a. the _____ fat +

b. the _____ fat -

?

0% fat

skim milk

4% fat

whole milk

2% fat

reduced-fat milk

Group Activity - Superlative

Instructions
Who in your group...?
1. Students form 2 groups.
2. Students interview the members in their group to answer the questions below.
3. Students in group 1 ask students in group 2 the same questions. Then switch.
(Teachers: Use this activity as class assessment.)

1 Who is wearing { the most / the fewest } rings today?

_____

2 Who drinks { the most / the least } coffee every morning?

_____

3 Who has { the most / the fewest } siblings?

_____

4 Who smiles { the most / the least } in class?

_____

EQUALITY

See Teacher's Manual

(Listen and repeat)
See the sample pictures on pages 2 and 3 and follow the instructions below.

Example

Which city has more traffic: London or New York?

<u>London</u> has as much traffic as <u>New York</u>.

or

<u>New York</u> has as much traffic as <u>London</u>.

Which city has fewer people: Tokyo or Paris?

<u>Paris</u> has fewer people than _____.

or

_____ doesn't have as many people as _____.

Oral Practice

(Elicit from the students)

1. London _____

2. Paris _____

3. _____

Equality

Comparative ⟶

As <u>many</u> *noun* as

Count Nouns

Eric has <u>as</u> <u>many</u> *dollars* <u>as</u> Peter.

or

Peter has <u>as</u> <u>many</u> *dollars* <u>as</u> Eric.

Peter

As <u>much</u> *noun* as

Noncount Nouns

Eric has <u>as</u> <u>much</u> *money* <u>as</u> Peter.

or

Peter has <u>as</u> <u>much</u> *money* <u>as</u> Eric.

Eric

Comparative ⟶

Negative verb + <u>as</u> <u>many</u> *noun* <u>as</u>

Count Nouns

Peter doesn't have <u>as</u> <u>many</u> *dollars* <u>as</u> Eric.

Peter

As <u>much</u> *noun* as

Noncount Nouns

Peter doesn't have <u>as</u> <u>much</u> *money* <u>as</u> Eric.

Eric

Group Oral Interaction

In groups, see the sample pictures on page 25 and complete the following dialogue.

In groups, see the sample pictures on page 25 and complete the following dialogue.

Example: **Comparative** ⟶ (=)

days

Milena has as many *days* as Gina to study for the final exam.

Gina has as many *days* as Milena to study for the final exam.

time

Milena has as much *time* as Gina to study for the final exam.

Gina has as much *time* as Milena to study for the final exam.

1.

bottles

Jennifer _____

Fred _____

water

Jennifer _____

Fred _____

2.   *students*

Class C _____

Class D _____

energy

Class C _____

Class D _____

3. *factories*

City D _____

City E _____

pollution

City D _____

City E _____

4. *songs*

Scott _____

Jayne _____

music

Scott _____

Jayne _____

24

Gina

Milena

Example

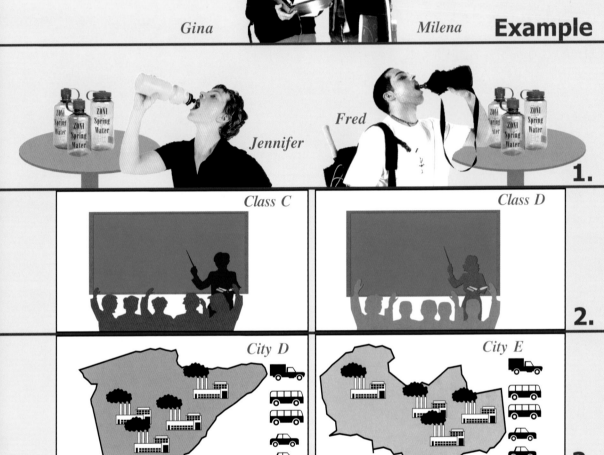

Jennifer

Fred

1.

Class C

Class D

2.

City D

City E

3.

Jayne

Scott

4.

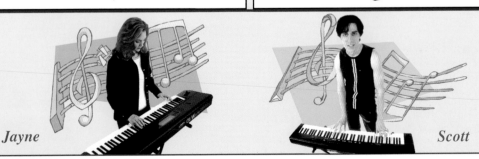

Group Oral Interaction

In groups, see the sample pictures on page 27 and complete
the following dialogue. *(Teachers: Assess Equality and Inequality here.)*

See Teacher's Manual

Example:
days

Comparative	

*Linda doesn't have **as many days as** Cindy to study for the final exam.*

time

*Linda doesn't have **as much time as** Cindy to study for the final exam.*

1. *bottles*

Mike

water

Mike

2. *students*

Class A

energy

Class A

3. *factories*

City A

pollution

City A

4. *songs*

Mary Ellen

music

Mary Ellen

26

Linda: I'm going to take the final exam **tomorrow**. I have to study tonight.

Cindy: My exam is **next week**. I still have time to study.

Example

Jennifer

Mike

1.

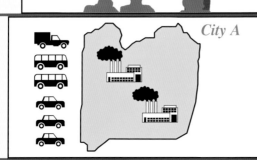

Class A

Class B

2.

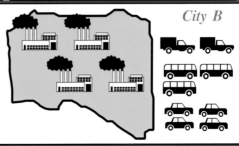

City A

City B

3.

Craig

Mary Ellen

4.

Homework

Make a complete sentence of equality or inequality based on the information below.

Example:

(eat / pasta)

Jean doesn't eat as much pasta as Anita.

Jean   Anita

1

(contain / food)

_____

a big refrigerator   a small refrigerator

2

(contain / alcohol)

_____

a bottle of wine   a bottle of beer

3

(have / children)

_____

Mr. and Mrs. Bagley

Mr. and Mrs. Lee

4

(have / flowers)

_____

green vase   red vase

28   ZONI ENGLISH SYSTEM ©

Homework

Make a complete sentence of <u>equality</u> or <u>inequality</u> based on the information below.

Example: Joe has a few problems. Mike has many problems.

Joe doesn't have as many problems as Mike.

1. I drink 8 glasses of water a day. You drink 8 glasses of water a day.

_____

2. Kim eats 2 sandwiches for lunch. Dora eats 1 sandwich for lunch.

_____

3. Ping listens to a lot of music. Lim Seok listens to some music.

_____

4. You drink 2 bottles of soda a day. I drink 3 bottles of soda a day.

_____

5. Carlos has many friends. Angela has many friends.

_____

6. Alaska gets a lot of snow. California gets a little snow.

_____

7. Frederick watches a little TV. Hee-Jung watches a little TV.

_____

8. Winston reads 2 hours a week. Hilda reads 10 hours a week.

_____

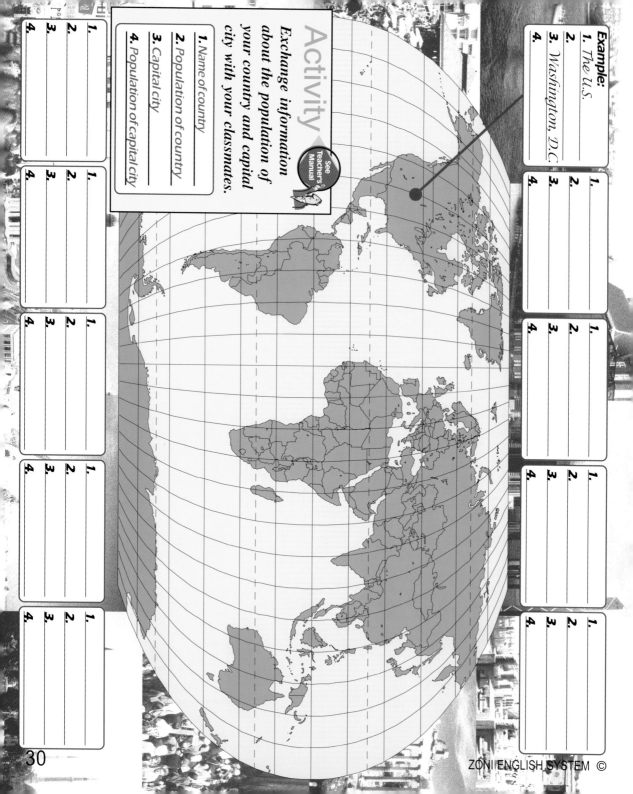

Example:
1. The U.S.
2.
3. Washington, D.C.
4.

See Teacher's Manual

Activity

Exchange information about the population of your country and capital city with your classmates.

1. Name of country
2. Population of country
3. Capital city
4. Population of capital city

1.
2.
3.
4.

1.
2.
3.
4.

1.
2.
3.
4.

1.
2.
3.
4.

1.
2.
3.
4.

1.
2.
3.
4.

1.
2.
3.
4.

1.
2.
3.
4.

1.
2.
3.
4.

1.
2.
3.
4.

1.
2.
3.
4.

Let's Chat!

With your partner, talk about…

1. where you are from.
2. where you live now.
3. the difference between your home city and the city where you are living now.
4. how you feel in the city where you are living now.

Let's Write

Write about your home city and the city where you are living now.

Dictation 1

(Listen to the teacher and write.)

1. _____

2. _____

3. _____

4. _____

5. _____

6. _____

7. _____

(Listen and repeat)

In is used with **centuries**, **years** and **months**.

Examples:

-Christopher Columbus discovered America **in** the 15th century.

-I came to the United States **in** 1990.

-New York is hot **in** August.

Christopher
Columbus
discovered
America.

On is used with **days** and **specific dates**.

Examples:

-I go to school only **on** Sundays.

-Jacky is going to see the doctor **on** January 3.

-My birthday is **on** November 13.

At is used with **specific times**.

Examples:

-I get up **at** 7:30 every morning.

-Sam asked me to come **at** 4:00 p.m.

-We eat lunch **at** noon every day.

In	Prepositions of time
	centuries, years, months

(Elicit from the students)
(Listen and repeat)

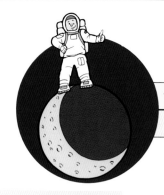

went to the moon
the 20th century

Example:

Men went to the moon in the 2oth century.

came to NY
1945

1. My grandfather _____

graduated from college
2001

2. George _____

visited Washington, D.C.
April

3. Marc and Tim _____

34

celebrate
December

4. We _____

saw the fireworks
July

5. Everyone _____

eat turkey
November

6. Americans _____

opened
1988

7. Zoni Language Centers _____

(Elicit from the students)
(Listen and repeat)

| play tennis |
| Saturdays |

Example:

I usually play tennis on Saturdays.

| start working |
| Mondays |

1. Chris _____

| study |
| Wednesdays |

2. Lisette _____

| dance |
| weekends |

3. Norma _____

go to sleep early

weekdays

4. Sandra _____

rest

Sundays

5. Bill _____

celebrate Independence Day

July 4

6. Americans _____

get presents

December 25

7. Some kids _____

At	Prepositions of time
	specific times

(Elicit from the students)
(Listen and repeat)

| Good | get up |
| morning! | 6:30 |

Example:

Janis always gets up at 6:30.

| drink |
| 8:00 a.m. |

1. Janis _____

| go |
| 9:30 a.m. |

2. Janis _____

| eat |
| 12:30 p.m. |

3. Janis _____

| come back |
| 6:00 p.m. |

4. Janis _____

| go to sleep |
| 10:00 p.m. |

5. Janis _____

Pair Practice

With a partner, answer the questions below.

*(Teachers: Assess prepositions of time: **in, on, at**)*

1. What time do you go to school?

_____

2. What time do you take a shower?

_____

3. When do you like to go dancing?

_____

4. When do you do your laundry?

_____

5. What time do you start doing your homework?

_____

6. When does your father call you?

_____

7. When does your country celebrate Independence Day?

_____

8. When do you celebrate your birthday?

_____

Homework
Rhonda's Story

Read the following story and fill in the blanks with the appropriate preposition (_in_, _on_, _at_.)

Rhonda Parker has three sisters: Pamela, Carla and Christy. Rhonda was born __in__ 1972, and she is the oldest. Pamela was born __in__ 1974. Carla was born __in__ 1980. Finally, Christy was born __in__ 1982, so she is the youngest. Although all the girls were born __in__ different years, by some strange coincidence, they were all born __on__ the same month. And, by an even stranger coincidence, Carla and Christy were born __in__ the same day!

Rhonda Parker

When the girls were growing up, their parents always celebrated their birthdays separately so that each girl would have her own special day. They tried to have each girl's party __on__ the exact day of her birth. With Rhonda and Pamela, there was no problem: they celebrated Rhonda's birthday __on__ November 3 and Pamela's birthday __on__ November 10. However, there was a big problem with Carla and Christy because both of their birthdays were _on_ November 20. Their parents came up with this solution: they had Carla's birthday party _on_ November 19, and they had Christy's birthday party _on_ November 21.

Now Rhonda, Pamela, Carla and Christy are grown up, married and have homes and children of their own. For this reason, the Parker family now has a different method of celebrating birthdays. All the sisters come home on Thanksgiving Day, which occurs _on_ the fourth Thursday _in_ November. The family celebrates Thanksgiving Day _on_ Thursday and then has one big birthday party for all the sisters two days later _on_ Saturday. Rhonda's parents say that the birth of their four daughters is their biggest reason to give thanks, so it is appropriate to have both celebrations _in_ the same month.

Homework
Reading Comprehension
In complete sentences, answer the following questions based on the reading.

1. Which sister was born in 1974?

Pamela was born in 1974

_____

2. Which sister was born in 1980?

Carla was born in 1980

_____

3. Which sister is the oldest?

Ronda is the oldest

4. Which sister is the youngest?

Chrisly is the youngest

5. Which two sisters were born on the same day?

Carla and Chrisly were born on the same day

6. Which day were they both born on?

november 18 They were born on november 20

7. When the sisters were growing up, did their parents have one big party for all of them?

they had one big party for all of them

8. Which sister was born on November 10?

Pamela was born on november 10

9. When does the Parker family celebrate the birthdays of the four sisters now?

two days after thanks givings

10. What other holiday does the family celebrate in November?

_____

42

(Listen and repeat)

In is used with <u>continents</u>, <u>countries</u>, <u>states</u> and <u>cities</u>.

Examples:

-Canada is **in** <u>North America</u>.

-My children live **in** <u>Venezuela</u>.

-It is hot **in** <u>Florida</u>.

-The White House is located **in** <u>Washington, D.C.</u>

On is used with <u>streets</u>, <u>avenues</u> and <u>floors</u>.

Examples:

-I live **on** <u>Washington Street</u>.

-My wife loves to go shopping **on** <u>Fifth Avenue</u>.

-Milton lives **on** <u>the second floor</u>.

At is used with <u>specific addresses</u>.

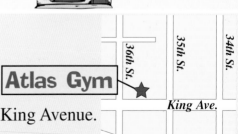

Examples:

-Mr. Hunk works out at <u>Atlas Gym</u> **at** <u>35-25</u> King Avenue.

-Ilsa would love to live **at** <u>20-13 White Street</u> in Forest Hills.

In	Prepositions of Place
	continents, countries, states and cities

(Elicit from the students)
(Listen and repeat)

Example:

live
Argentina

Jose-Luis lives in Argentina.

study
Beijing

studies

1. Yilian ~~studys~~ *in beijing*

teach
South Korea

2. Kee-Yong *teaches in south korea*

met Steven
Mexico City

meets

3. Jacky ~~meets~~ *steven in Mexico City*

bought dolls
Russia

4. Elena *bought dolls in Russia*

44

speak
Montreal

5. They _speak french in Montreal_

visited his friend
California

6. Ken _visited his friend in California_

drive
Rome

7. We _drive in Rome_

live
South America

8. Carmen _lives in South America_

be
North America

9. Mexico _is in North America_

(Elicit from the students)
(Listen and repeat)

Example:

saw
2nd Avenue and 54th Street

Jacky saw Steven on 2nd Avenue and 54th Street.

live
54th Street

1. Hank *lives on 54th street*

had
the highway

2. She *had an accident on the highway*

is
the first floor

3. Our apartment *is on the first floor*

caught
Fifth Avenue

4. Takeru *caught a taxi on fifth avenue*

46

At

Prepositions of Place

specific addresses

(Elicit from the students)
(Listen and repeat)

Example:

work
36 Bergenline Avenue

I work at 36 Bergenline Avenue.

live
28-04 Broadway

1. Marilyn *lives at 28-04 Broadway*

exercise
90-17 Fifth Avenue

2. Brisy *exercises at 90-17 fifth Avenue*

eat lunch
80-20 64th Street

3. Pat and Marcela *eat lunch at 802064th Street*

go to school
78-14 Roosevelt Avenue

4. Marty *go to school at 7814 Roosevelt Avenue*

Pair Practice

With a partner, answer the questions below. Use your imagination.
(Teachers: Assess prepositions of place: __in__, __on__, __at__)

1. Where do you live? **(at)**

I live at 31-28   47th street

2. Where did you get the bus? **(on)**

I take the bus on Broadway

3. Where does your brother work? **(at)**

_____

4. Where did you find the best beach? **(in)**

_____

5. Where is your apartment? **(on)**

_____

6. Where does Mr. Kim like to jog? **(on)**

_____

Fill in the blanks with _in_, _on_ or _at_.

Victor is a man who has made most of his dreams come true. He arrived _____ the United States when he was 26 years old. First he lived _____ Brooklyn, but afterwards he lived _____ Corona, Queens. In the beginning, he was a little scared because he didn't know many people in his apartment building. He didn't speak much English, but he learned to say, "I live _____ 33-90 Grove Street." Later on, he found a job _____ Queens. He worked in a travel agency. His office was _____ the second floor. After he learned his job well, he opened his own business _____ 12-42 Woodside Avenue. He works a lot of hours, but he still wants to study more English and computers at Zoni Language Centers _____ Queens. He is also planning to buy his own home _____ a city that is close to his business.

Homework
Reading Comprehension

In complete sentences, answer the following questions based on the reading.

1. What is the name of the person in the reading?

_____

2. How old was Victor when he came to New York?

_____

3. Where did he live first?

_____

4. How did he feel at the beginning?

_____

5. Did he know how to speak English well?

_____

6. Where did he get his first job?

_____

7. Where does he want to study English?

_____

8. What is he planning to buy now?

_____

9. Where would he like to buy his house?

_____

10. When you came to New York, was your experience similar to Victor's experience?

_____

Lesson 2
FREQUENCY

FREQUENCY

See Teacher's Manual

(Listen and repeat)

HOW OFTEN DO YOU...?

every minute   every day
once a day   once a week
twice a day   twice a week
three times a day   three times a year

Exercise A

Answer the following "a" questions on your own.
Then interview your partner ...

a) How often do you...?   *b) How often does your partner...?*

1. go to school?

a)_____   b)_____

2. exercise?

a)_____   b)_____

3. get a general check up?

a)_____   b)_____

4. brush your teeth?

a)_____   b)_____

52

5. see your dentist?

a) _____   *b)* _____

6. take your vitamins?

a) _____   *b)* _____

7. eat fruit?

a) _____   *b)* _____

8. eat vegetables?

a) _____   *b)* _____

9. eat steak?

a) _____   *b)* _____

10. meditate?

a) _____   *b)* _____

Exercise B

Report your answers to the class.

Example

I exercise three times a week. Muhammed, my classmate, doesn't exercise at all.

1. _____

2. _____

3. _____

Expressions of Frequency

every hour
every day
once a day
twice a week
three times a month
four times a year

(Elicit from the students)
(Listen and repeat)

Example

The doctor said I should take this medicine **every eight hours**.

(The doctor said I should take this medicine <u>three times a day</u>.)

RX
TAKE ONE
TABLET BY
MOUTH THREE
TIMES DAILY
AFTER MEALS.

1

My mother goes grocery shopping **every Saturday**.

(My mother goes grocery shopping _____.)

2

Cherry blossoms bloom **every spring** in Japan.

(Cherry blossoms bloom _____.)

3

Eric goes to the gym on **Tuesdays and Saturdays**.

(Eric goes to the gym _____.)

54

Oral Practice
(Elicit from the students)
(Listen and repeat)

1

How often does she do laundry?

She does laundry _____.

S	M	T	W	T	F	S
1	2	3	4	5	6	7
8	9	10	11	12	13	14
15	16	17	18	19	20	21
22	23	24	25	26	27	28
29	30					

2

Does he coach kid's soccer **every evening**?

No, he doesn't. He coaches _____.

Wednesday

Saturday

Sunday

3

When do they eat out?

They eat out _____ because that's payday!

I can't wait until Friday every week.

Me, neither.

4

SUN	MON	TUE	WED	THU	FRI	SAT
OFF	English	English	English	English	Math	Math

Does he study English **every night**?

No, he doesn't. He studies _____.

5

How often should I go to the dentist?

You should go _____.

6

Does your sister clean her room **every week**?

Yes, she does. She cleans it_____.

7

How often do you eat lobster?

We eat lobster _____. We love lobster,
but it's very expensive.

I was dreaming about eating lobster on our special day!

Happy anniversary, honey.

Frequency

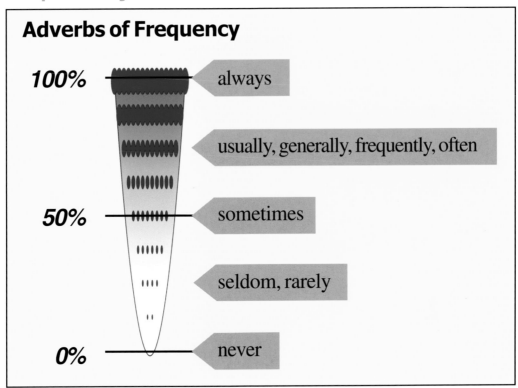

Adverbs of Frequency

100% ━━━ always

usually, generally, frequently, often

50% ─── sometimes

seldom, rarely

0% ━━ never

Examples
(Listen and repeat)

▶ CASE 1 > **adverb + verb**	▶ CASE 2 > **be verb + adverb**
I **always** take public transportation.	Juan is **always** late.
I **usually** take the train.	He's **usually** a half-hour late.
I **sometimes** take the bus. or **Sometimes,** I take the bus (sometimes).	He's **sometimes** fifteen minutes late. or **Sometimes,** he's fifteen minutes late (**sometimes**).
I **never** take a taxi.	He's **never** on time.

Group Oral Interaction

In groups, answer the questions below using the adverbs of frequency found on page 57.

1. How often does Philip cook?

_____

2. How often does Aki watch TV?

_____

3. How often is George in a good mood?

_____

4. How often do Peter and his wife play golf on weekends?

_____

5. How often do Mary and John go out on weekends?

_____

Group Oral Interaction

See Teacher's Manual

In groups, ask and answer questions about all of you. Use adverbs of frequency or expressions of frequency in your answers.

(Teachers: Assess adverbs and expressions of frequency here.)

Example:

Do you exercise a lot?

Yes, I do. I exercise every morning.

1. How often do you watch TV?

_____

2. When do you buy groceries?

_____

3. Do you visit your friends a lot?

_____

4. How often do you work overtime?

_____

5. Are you always late for class?

_____

6. What time do you get up on Sundays?

_____

7. Do you take public transportation?

_____

8. Are you romantic?

_____

9. How frequently do you listen to music?

_____

10. Do you write letters to your friends in your country?

_____

Homework

Answer these questions about you. Use adverbs of frequency or expressions of frequency in your answers.

Examples:

How often do you listen to the radio in English?

I listen to the radio in English sometimes.

Do you go to the movies a lot?

Yes, I do. I go to the movies every weekend.

1. How often do you read the newspaper in English?

_____

2. When do you do your homework?

_____

3. Do you speak English outside class a lot?

_____

4. How often do you work on weekends?

_____

5. Are you always on time for work?

_____

6. What time do you go to sleep?

_____

7. Do you take the subway to school?

_____

8. Are you shy?

_____

9. How frequently do you surf the Internet?

_____

10. Do you stay in contact with your friends and family in your country?

_____

62

Once in a Blue Moon

Today, the expression "once in a blue moon" means that something does not happen very often. But where did the term "blue moon" come from? And does the moon really turn blue? The history of the expression reveals two meanings.

The Old Meaning

A year has four seasons: winter, summer, spring and fall. A "full" moon is when we can see the complete moon from earth. Each season usually has only three full moons, but once in a while a season has four. As far back as the early 1800s, the people who wrote the farmer's almanac (a guide for farmers planting crops) used a different color ink to mark the fourth full moon to occur in a season that had four full moons. It is thought that they used blue ink to mark the fourth full moon; therefore, this moon became known as the "blue moon."

Today's Meaning

Somehow in the 1980s, the expression changed to refer to the second full moon to occur in any calendar month. Because a full moon normally occurs every 29.5 days, and the 12 months of our calendar year have either 30 or 31 days (except February, which has 28 or 29 days), two full moons seldom occur in the same month. On average, a "blue moon" occurs approximately every 2.5 years.

One Extra Note

Although the moon never turns blue, there are times when the moon can *appear* bluish to us here on earth. For example, when a huge volcanic eruption throws a lot of debris into the atmosphere, the debris can block certain types of the moon's light rays from reaching the earth. When this happens, the moon can appear bluish in color when viewed from earth.

Homework
Reading Comprehension

Answer "T" (True), "F" (False), or "NI" (No Information)

1. Today, the expression "once in a blue moon" means that something happens twice in one month.

☐ T   ☐ F   ☐ NI

2. The term "full moon" means that we can see the complete moon from earth.

☐ T   ☐ F   ☐ NI

3. The last blue moon occurred in 2004.

☐ T   ☐ F   ☐ NI

4. According to the older definition, a blue moon referred to the fourth moon to occur in a season that had four full moons.

☐ T   ☐ F   ☐ NI

5. According to the 1980s' definition, a blue moon refers to the second full moon to occur in the same calendar month.

☐ T   ☐ F   ☐ NI

6. Volcanic eruptions on the moon cause it to turn blue in color at certain times of the year.

☐ T   ☐ F   ☐ NI

7. The term "blue moon" appears in the lyrics of several songs.

☐ T   ☐ F   ☐ NI

8. Although the moon never really changes color, it can sometimes appear bluish when viewed from earth.

☐ T   ☐ F   ☐ NI

Still	the continuation of an opinion, a condition or an action
Anymore	the termination (or change) of an opinion, a condition or an action

Examples (Listen and repeat)

1

Does Pablito still drink coffee?

Yes, he **still** drinks coffee.

No, he doesn't drink coffee anymore.

2

Is Ms. Conte still single?

Yes, she's **still** single.

No, she's not single anymore.
(Now, she's married.)

3

Do you still smoke?

Yes, I **still** smoke.

No, I don't smoke anymore.

4

Is Bill still stealing from others?

Yes, he's **still** stealing.

No, he isn't stealing anymore.
(Now, he's in jail.)

Group Oral Interaction

In groups, make sentences with <u>still</u> and <u>anymore</u> using the graphics below.

1. Do you still bite your fingernails?

Yes, _____

No, _____

2. Is it still raining outside?

Yes, _____

No, _____

3. Is Caroline still talking on the phone?

bla bla bla...

Yes, _____

No, _____

4. Does Leo still wear glasses?

Yes, _____

No, _____

Student A asks a question or answers using <u>still</u> or <u>anymore</u> based on the graphics below.

1

A: _____ ?

(Raymond / work)

2

A: _____ .

(Daniela / study / midnight)

3

A: _____ ?

(Fred and Anne / love)

4

Now!

A: _____ .

(Merce / be / pregnant)

5

A: _____ ?

(Ronda / use / typewriter)

Student B
The Simple Present Tense

Student B asks a question or answers using <u>still</u> or <u>anymore</u> based on the graphics below.

---

1 Retired!

B: _____.
(Raymond / work)

2

B: _____?
(Daniela / study / midnight)

3

B: _____.
(Fred and Anne / love)

---

4 *10 days ago*

B: _____?
(Merce / be / pregnant)

5

B: _____.
(Ronda / use / typewriter)

ZONI ENGLISH SYSTEM ©

Your Life

Exercise A

Write about your life **5 years ago**. Then compare that list with **today**.

5 YEARS AGO	TODAY
1. *had long hair*	*have long hair*
2. *was timid*	*am not timid*
3.	
4.	
5.	
6.	
7.	

Exercise B

No writing. Based on the information above, talk about and share your life with your group. Use **still** or **anymore** in your conversation.

Homework

Based on the information above, write sentences using **still** or **anymore**.

1. *I still have long hair.*

2. I don't dance tango animore

3. I dond smoke anymore

4.

5.

6.

7.

"Used to" plus a verb indicates a habitual opinion, condition or action. "Still" indicates a continuation of a habitual opinion, condition or action. "Anymore" indicates a termination (or change) of a habitual opinion, condition or action.

Examples (Listen and repeat)

1 Kim used to work in a restaurant in her country, but she doesn't work in a restaurant anymore. *(Now, she works in an office.)*

Gislaine used to work in a restaurant in her country, **and** she **still** works in a restaurant now.

2 Claire used to have long hair when she was a child, but she doesn't have long hair anymore. *(Now, she has short hair.)*

Andrea used to have long hair when she was a child, **and** she **still** has long hair now.

3 Eric and Amy used to be in love when they were in college, but they aren't in love anymore.

Jack and Pamela used to be in love when they were in college, **and** they are **still** in love now.

4 I used to think the guitar was difficult to play, but I don't think so anymore.

Leo used to think the guitar was difficult to play, **and** he **still** thinks so.

5 Freddie used to smoke two packs of cigarettes a day, but he doesn't smoke at all anymore.

John used to smoke two packs of cigarettes a day, **and** he **still** smokes two packs a day now.

Still
Anymore

Student A

The Present Progressive Tense

Student A asks a question or answers using <u>still</u> or <u>anymore</u> based on the graphics below.

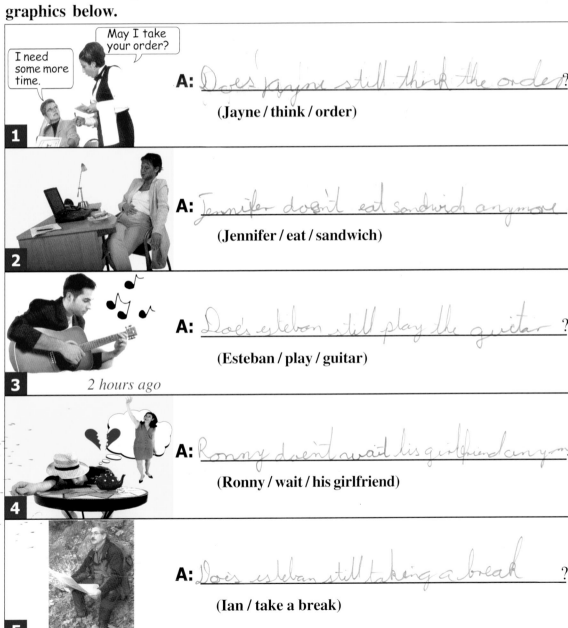

1

A: Does Jayne still think the order?

(Jayne / think / order)

2

A: Jennifer doesn't eat sandwich anymore.

(Jennifer / eat / sandwich)

3 *2 hours ago*

A: Does esteban still play the guitar?

(Esteban / play / guitar)

4

A: Ronny doesn't wait his girlfriend anymore

(Ronny / wait / his girlfriend)

5

A: Does esteban still taking a break?

(Ian / take a break)

ZONI ENGLISH SYSTEM ©

71

Student B asks a question or answers using <u>still</u> or <u>anymore</u> based on the graphics below.

1

umm...

B: Jayne is still think the order .

(Jayne / think / order)

2

B: is Jennifer still eat the sandwich?

(Jennifer / eat / sandwich)

3

Now!

B: Esteban is still playing the guitar .

(Esteban / play / guitar)

4

B: is Ronny still waiting for his girlfriend?

(Ronny / wait / his girlfriend)

5

B: Ian doesn't take a break anymore .

(Ian / take a break)

ZONI ENGLISH SYSTEM ©

Write and Share

ABOUT YOU

Write and share your information. Use one example each for <u>still</u> and <u>anymore</u>.

1. _I don't drive my car anymore_

2. _I still play soccer in Ny_

ABOUT YOUR PARTNER

Listen to your partner and write his or her information.

Partner's name: _Carlota_

1. _she's doesn't Ride a bicicle anymore_

2. _she still cook the dinner everiday_

I used to ...

Write personal examples with "used to" + base verb. Use sentences in the negative or affirmative.

1. _I used to go to the college but I don't anymore_

2. _I used to drive a car but I don't anymor_

3. _I use to play soccer in my contry but I don't play anymore_

4. _I use to work in my contry but I study english here_

Group Oral Interaction

See Teacher's Manual

In groups, ask one another what you used to do and what you did not use to do. *(Teachers: Assess **used to** with **still** and **not anymore**.)*

Did you use to...

wake up early?

wake up late?

- Used to ...
- Don't anymore
- Because ...

Pair Practice-Part I

Follow the model below. Switch roles and repeat.

A: I used to smoke, but I don't anymore.

B: Why not?

A: Because it's bad for my health.

before  now

B: *Why not?*

A: I used to ...

1. take the bus every day, but I...
2. listen to rap music, but I...
3. go out with Cristina, but I...

A: Because ...

now I have a car.

now I prefer jazz.

we broke up.

Pair Practice-Part II

Follow the model above, but this time, create information for the blank spaces. Switch roles and repeat.

A: I used to ...

1. drink a lot of coffee, but I...
2. get up at 7:30, but I...
3. play football but
4. smoke cigarettes but

B: *Why not?*

A: Because ...

it's bad for my health

now I work in the afternoon

now I'm too busy.

it's a bad habit.

Homework

Answer in the negative form.

1. Do they still work at the hospital?

_____

2. Is the child still hungry?

_____

3. Is it still raining?

_____

4. Are Pamela and Bill still going out?

_____

5. Does Emma still bite her fingernails?

_____

Exercise B

Personal Information. Answer yes or no to these questions about you.

1. Are you still taking course 103?

_____

2. Are you still taking course 204?

_____

3. Is your family still in your country?

_____

4. Do you still play with toys?

_____

5. Do you still think that the train and bus schedules are confusing?

_____

6. Do you still think that English is difficult?

_____

Exercise C

Make a question.

1.

_____?

Yes, I'm still doing my homework.

2.

_____?

No, we're not homesick anymore.

3.

_____?

    No, Yukio doesn't live in Japan anymore.

4.

_____?

    Yes, Igor's brother still works at the United Nations.

5.

_____?

    Yes, he still likes rock and roll.

6.

_____?

    No, she doesn't think John is handsome anymore.

Exercise D

Give examples of some things you used to think or do that you don't anymore. Tell why you don't.

    Example: I used to eat a lot of ice cream, but I don't anymore because it's too fattening.

1._____

2._____

3._____

Dictation 2A

See Teacher's Manual

(Listen to the teacher and write.)

1. _____

2. _____

3. _____

4. _____

5. _____

6. _____

7. _____

MODALS – Part I: Review Summary
Group Work

In groups of three, write example sentences for each modal verb below.

may	can	should
-Formal request/permission (in public situations)	-Ability -Request (informal)	-Advice/recommendation
1._____	1._____	1._____
2._____	2._____	2._____

have to/must	will	must not
-Obligation/necessity	-Future promise or prediction	-Prohibition
1._____	1._____	1._____
2._____	2._____	2._____

Which modal is correct?

[*- may - can - have to/must - must not - should*]

(Elicit from the students)

(Listen and repeat)

This modal indicates ***obligation***.	This modal indicates ***advice***.
Onur bought a house, and now he _____ pay a $2,000-a-month mortgage.	Susan would like to lose some weight. She _____ go to the gym.
This modal indicates ***informal request/friends & family***.	This modal indicates ***prohibition***.
We need to talk. _____ I come over right now?	My father is very ill, and his doctor told him that he _____ smoke.

This modal indicates ___necessity___.	This modal indicates ___ability___.
To have energy you _____ consume a lot of carbohydrates.	My friend is a talented musician. He _____ play the guitar, the piano and the drums.

Group Oral Interaction

In groups, give examples of each modal. Each member of the group must give an example for each modal.

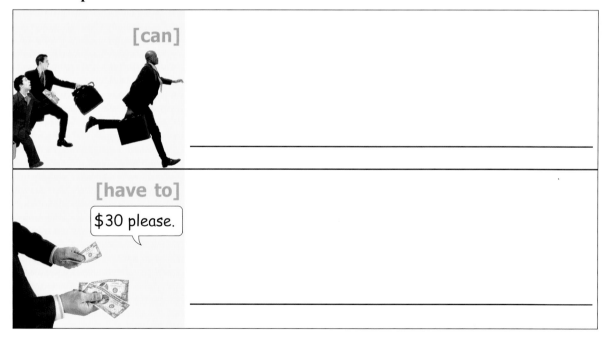

[can]

[have to]

$30 please.

[should]

_____

[must not]

_____

[can]

_____

[will]

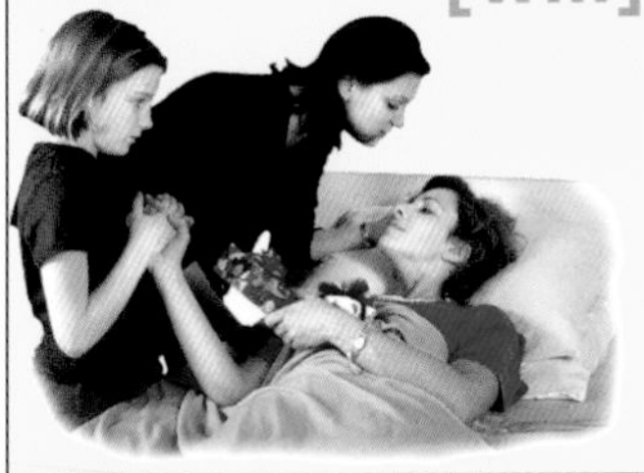

_____

[may]

Teacher!

_____

Homework

Reading Comprehension

Write answers to the following questions based on the dialogue.

1. What are Vickie and her co-worker, Ann, doing?

_____

2. Why is Vickie very hungry?

_____

3. What does Vickie always drink in the morning?

_____

4. Which meal did Ann's doctor tell her never to skip?

_____

5. Did Vickie use to eat breakfast?

_____

6. Why doesn't Vickie prepare breakfast anymore?

_____

7. Does Vickie usually go to sleep earlier now than she used to before her schedule changed?

_____

8. Which meal does Vickie still think is important?

_____

9. What would Vickie rather do: sleep later or get up earlier to make breakfast?

_____

Lesson 3

THE PRESENT PERFECT

THE PRESENT PERFECT

What Have You Done Recently?

See Teacher's Manual

1. _I have seen 2 movies recently._

2. _____

3. _____

4. _____

5. _____

6. _____

7. _____

8. _____

9. _____

10. _____

Recently/Lately

An action that occurred a short time ago in the past where the specific time is not mentioned.

Examples

(Listen and repeat)
(Elicit from the students)

1
Have you seen any good movies lately?

Yes, I've seen several good ones lately.

2
Have you been to the dentist **recently**?

No, I haven't been to the dentist **recently**. I must go soon.

3
Has Miguel flown to Colombia **recently**?

No, he hasn't flown there **recently**.

4
Have the students practiced their English much lately?

Yes, they've practiced a lot lately.

5
Have you gone shopping for clothes lately?

No, I haven't gone shopping for clothes lately.

6
Have you read any mystery novels **recently**?

No, I haven't read any mystery novels **recently**.

Group Oral Interaction

In groups, make a question and answer it using the information below. Select a correct information word: <u>what</u>, <u>where</u>, <u>who(m)</u>, <u>how much</u>, <u>how many</u>.

Examples: **Q:** *What has Miguel driven lately?*

A: *He's driven a new SUV.*
Miguel/drive/lately

Q: *Where have you traveled recently?*

A: *I've traveled to California.*
(You / travel / recently)

1. Q: _____ ?

A: _____ .   *Frank   Karen*
(Karen / kiss / recently)

Happy birthday Mary!

2. Q: _____ ?

Philip

A: _____ .
(Philip / send / lately)

3. Q: _____ ?

A: _____ .
(They / donate / recently)

4. Q: _____?

A: _____.

(You / drink / lately)

5. Q: _____?

A: _____.

Anne   Samuel

(Samuel / dance with / recently)

6. Q: _____?

A: _____.

Cindy   Paul

(Cindy and Paul / share / lately)

7. Q: _____?

A: _____.

(The students / study English / recently)

8. Q: _____?

A: _____.

(You / rent / recently)

Interviews

Interview A

One student interviews six students asking them what they **have done** lately or recently. The student records the answers in the book.
*(Teachers: Assess the present perfect with **lately** and **recently** here.)*

What have you done lately (or recently)?

1._____

2._____

3._____

4._____

5._____

6._____

Interview B

One student interviews six students asking them what they **have _not_ done** lately or recently. The student records the answers in the book.

What have you not done lately (or recently)?

1._____

2._____

3._____

4._____

5._____

6._____

ZONI ENGLISH SYSTEM ©

Homework

Write about things your friends, relatives, classmates or co-workers **have** or **have not done** lately or recently.

Example: *My brother, Luis, has not called me lately.*

1._____

2._____

3._____

4._____

5._____

Exercise B

Make an information question based on the highlighted words, using **what**, **where**, **who(m)**, **how much**, **how many**.

1. Q: _____?
   A: I've eaten Chinese food recently.

2. Q: _____?
   A: I've danced at the nightclub recently.

3. Q: _____?
   A: Lisa has not seen her boyfriend recently.

4. Q: _____?
   A: Paul hasn't drunk much beer lately.

5. Q: _____?
   A: The students have had a lot of tests lately.

Yes,...already	Actions completed before now
No,...yet	Actions not completed before now

Examples (Listen and repeat)

1.

Has Lucy Roberts been to the bank yet?

No, she hasn't been to the bank yet.

2.

Has Lucy Roberts cashed her check yet?

Yes, she's **already** cashed her check.

or

Yes, she's cashed her check **already**.

Taxi!

July 10, 2004
Lucy Roberts | $ 100.00
PAY TO THE ORDER OF
One hundred and 00/100 /100 DOLLARS
Memo _____ ZoniGroup

Pair Practice

With your partner, ask and answer questions following the examples.

Examples	**Q:** *Have you brushed your teeth yet?* **A:** *Yes, I've already brushed them.*
	Q: *Have you seen the Statue of Liberty yet?* **A:** *No, I haven't seen it yet.*
1	**Q:** _____ yet? **A:** No, _____.
2	**Q:** _____ yet? **A:** Yes, _____.
accounting psychology math **3**	**Q:** _____ yet? **A:** No, _____.
My pleasure. Thank you for lunch. I had a good time. Check **4**	**Q:** _____ yet? **A:** Yes, _____.

Pair Practice

An Lee has a busy schedule today. She has made a check mark [√] in front of the errands she has already run. With your partner, ask and answer the following questions based on the list.
*(Teachers: Assess **Yes,...already** and **No,...yet** here.)*

See Teacher's Manual

Pair Practice

Things to Do

☑ **Cash paycheck at the bank**	☐ **Wash her car**
☑ **Buy groceries at the supermarket**	☐ **Put gas in the car**
☑ **Bring the children to school**	☐ **Pick up the children from school**
☑ **Take the dirty clothes to the dry cleaners**	☐ **Make dinner**
☑ **Return 3 books to the library**	☐ **Call mother to see how she is feeling**

Examples

{ Has she called her mother yet?
  No, she hasn't called her yet.

{ Has she cashed her paycheck yet?
  Yes, she's already cashed it.

1. Has she taken the dirty clothes to the dry cleaners yet?

_____

2. Has she returned the books to the library yet?

_____

3. Has she made dinner yet?

_____

4. Has she put gas in the car yet?

_____

5. Has she brought the children to school yet?

_____

6. Has she washed her car yet?

_____

7. Has she bought groceries yet?

_____

8. Has she picked up the children from school yet?

_____

Homework

Answer the questions below with the present perfect in the affirmative or the negative. Use the information in parentheses to help you.

1. Have you eaten lunch yet? (**I went to the deli with my friends.**)

_____

2. Has Maria gotten married yet? (**Her wedding is next month.**)

_____

3. Have those students finished course 204 yet? (**They are in course 205 now.**)

_____

4. Have you taken out the garbage yet? (**I'll do it right now.**)

_____

5. Have you heard the new Celine Dion CD yet? (**I think it's wonderful.**)

_____

Just

An action that occurred a very short time ago in the past where the specific time is not mentioned.

Examples
(Listen and repeat)

1 Igor and Svetlana have just gotten married.

2 Flight 202 has just taken off.

Bon Voyage!

3 Mr. Peterson has just finished eating dinner in a restaurant.

Right away, sir.

Waitress, check, please.

4 Two students have just volunteered to perform a dialogue.

What's your last name?

My last name is Arabaci.

5 Cristina has just fallen asleep.

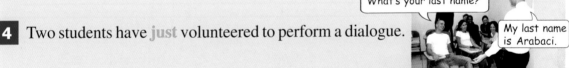

6 Tomas has just caught a fish.

Adverbs of Frequency

ever (=at any time)
never
sometimes
always
seldom
often

(Listen and repeat)
(Elicit from the students)

1

Have you ever **been** to Brazil?

No, I **have** never **been** to Brazil.

2

Has your wife ever **seen** the children fighting?

My wife **has** sometimes **seen** the children fighting.

3

Have you and your sister ever **spoken** in English?

We **have** always **spoken** in English.

4

Have John and Steven ever **forgotten** to call you?

John and Steven **have** seldom **forgotten** to call me.

5

Have you ever **told** your friends to take it easy?

I **have** often **told** my friends to take it easy.

How often:
Frequency of occurrence

every day
every week
once a week
twice a month
never

(Listen and repeat)
(Elicit from the students)

1

How often **have** you **practiced** Karate lately?

I**'ve practiced** every day.

2

How often **has** Mrs. Kim **gone** grocery shopping lately?

She**'s gone** twice a week lately.

3

How often **has** Sam **gotten** a speeding ticket?

He**'s gotten** a speeding ticket once a year.

4

How often **have** you **visited** your parents since 1998?

I**'ve visited** them twice a year since 1998.

5

How often **has** the baby **been** sick this winter?

She**'s been** sick once a month this winter.

6

How often **have** they **fallen** asleep at the movies?

They**'ve never fallen** asleep at the movies.

7

How often **has** Chantal **taken** a vacation?

She**'s taken** a vacation once in a blue moon.

Pair Practice

With a partner, ask and answer the questions below.

(Teachers: Assess adverbs of frequency and frequency of occurrence here.)

Pair Practice

1. How often have you gotten to school late? **(never)**

I _____

2. How often has Martha sent you letters? **(twice a year)**

She _____

3. How often have you and your girlfriend gone to the beach? **(every summer)**

We _____

4. How often have you gotten to your job early? **(always)**

I _____

5. How often has Mr. Dixon made bad decisions? **(seldom)**

He _____

6. How often have Mike and Tina jogged in Central Park this summer? **(every morning)**

They _____

How many times:
Repetition of occurrence

once
twice
three times
a few times
several times
many times
too many times
never

(Listen and repeat)
(Elicit from the students)

1
How many times **have** you **seen** that movie?

I**'ve seen** it five times.

2
How many times **has** she **fallen** in love with the wrong man?

She**'s fallen** in love with the wrong man too many times.

3
How many times **have** they **played** tennis this summer?

They**'ve played** tennis several times this summer.

4
How many times **has** that baseball team **lost** this season?

They**'ve lost** only once this season.

5
How many times **have** you **called** your family this week?

I**'ve called** them a few times this week.

6
How many times **have** you and Gabriella **played** the lottery this week?

We**'ve played** it twice this week: once on Wednesday and again on Friday.

7
How many times **has** your brother **borrowed** money from you this month?

He**'s borrowed** money from me once this month.

Pair Practice

With a partner, complete the dialogues according to the graphics.

(Teachers: Assess repetition of occurrence here.)

See Teacher's Manual

Pair Practice

1

A: Have you ever_____?

B: Yes, _____.

A: How many times have you_____?

B: _____ many times.

2

A: Has your sister ever_____?

B: Yes, _____.

A: How many times_____?

B: _____ twice.

3

A: Have the students ever_____?

B: Yes, _____.

A: How many times_____?

B: _____ a few times.

4

A: Have your parents ever_____?

B: Yes, _____.

A: How often _____?

B: _____twice a year.

110

5

A: Have you ever _____?

B: Yes, I have _____.

A: How many times _____?

B: _____ many times.

6

A: Have you and your wife ever _____?

B: Yes, we _____.

A: How often _____?

B: _____ very often.

7

A: Have your friends ever _____?

B: Yes, they _____.

A: How many times _____?

B: _____ a few times.

8

I'm giving you an exam today.

A: Has your teacher ever _____?

B: Yes, he _____.

A: How many times _____?

B: _____ several times.

<table>
<tr><td>**for**</td><td rowspan="2">-Used with the present perfect to express an action that began in the past and continues into the present.</td></tr>
<tr><td>**since**</td></tr>
</table>

Examples
(Listen and repeat)

1 **I've** shopp**ed** **since** 9 o'clock.

2 **You've** liv**ed** in New York **for** 10 years.

3 **He's** stud**ied** Karate **since** he was 20 years old.

4 **She's** paint**ed** watercolors **for** 15 years.

114

5 **It's** rain**ed** for 3 hours.

6 **We've** **stood** at attention **since** last night.

7 **You've** surf**ed** the Net for 2 hours.

8 **They've** **gotten** along with each other **for** over fifty years.

Pair Practice

| **Since** | - To indicate **when an action began** |
| **For** | - To indicate **the duration of an action** |

Examples

I've studied English at Zoni **since last summer**.

Natasha and Ilhan have studied English at Zoni **for 6 months**.

With a partner, fill in the blanks using the appropriate word, <u>since</u> or <u>for</u>.

1. It has snowed in Alaska _____ last week.

2. Karla has studied there _____ 7 months.

3. Mr. Jones has discussed the topic _____ two hours.

4. We have lived in New York _____ last summer.

5. Jake has worked in the pharmacy _____ 1 year.

6. Wanda has looked for a bigger apartment _____ last June.

7. Jean-Pierre and Françoise have danced _____ almost 4 hours!

8. Sophia has not had any chocolate _____ December.

9. Donna has expected to hear from you _____ several months.

10. John and Kelly have stayed at the Fontainebleau hotel _____ they arrived.

ZONI ENGLISH SYSTEM ©

Let's Practice!
Irregular Verbs-Past Participles
(Listen and repeat)
(Elicit from the students)
Close your books and follow your teacher's instructions.

See Teacher's Manual

Verb	Past Participle	Verb	Past Participle
become	*become*	leave	*left*
begin	*begun*	let	*let*
blow		lie	
bring		lose	
buy		make	
catch		meet	
come		read	
cost		ride	
cut		run	
do		say	
drink		see	
drive		sell	
eat		send	
fall		sing	
feel		sit	
fight		sleep	
find		speak	
fit		spend	
fly		stand	
forget		swim	
get		take	
get up		teach	
give		understand	
go		wake	
grow		wear	
have		win	
know		write	

Dictation 3

(Listen to the teacher and write.)

1. _____

2. _____

3. _____

4. _____

5. _____

6. _____

7. _____

Homework
University Life

**Christine is a university student. She is in her room doing her homework.
The telephone has just rung. It's her boyfriend, Jack.**

Christine: Hello?

Jack: Hi, honey. How's it going?

Christine: Not great. I'm up to my neck in homework, but I'm really glad you called. I need a little break.

Jack: Haven't you finished your homework yet? I thought you'd be done by now.

Christine: No, unfortunately. I'm still working on it. I've already finished my math, but I've just started my chemistry.

Jack: I was calling to invite you to dinner tomorrow night. We haven't seen each other much recently, and I miss you.

Christine: I miss you, too. I haven't seen you or any of my friends much lately because I spend so much time doing homework or studying for exams. But, I've told myself many times that some day all this hard work will pay off.

Jack: It will. So, about dinner—do you think you can make it?

Christine: I'd love to go out tomorrow night, but I can't unless I finish this chemistry homework tonight.

Jack: Well, maybe I can come over and help you with it. I haven't studied chemistry since high school, but I used to get straight A's in all my classes, and I think I remember most of it. Besides you've helped me once a week with my English Literature classes for two semesters, so now it's my turn to help you.

Christine: Well, I really would appreciate some help tonight. I haven't studied chemistry since high school, either. The problem is that I wasn't good at it then, and I'm still not good at it now.

Jack: What if I come over in about a half hour?

Christine: A half hour sounds good.

Jack: Do you want me to bring some doughnuts or something to eat?

Christine: No thanks. I made some chocolate chip cookies this afternoon, and I've just finished brewing some strong coffee, so your brains are all I need.

Jack: Well then, my brains and I will be there in thirty minutes.

Christine: Great. I'll see you in a bit. Bye, honey.

Jack: Bye.

Homework
Reading Comprehension

In complete sentences, answer the following questions based on the reading.

1. What is Christine having trouble with?

_____

2. Who is Jack?

_____

3. Has Christine finished her homework yet?

_____

4. Have Christine and Jack seen each other a lot recently?

_____

5. Has Christine seen any of her other friends lately?

_____

6. What has Christine spent so much time doing lately?

_____

7. What has Christine told herself many times?

_____

8. How often has Christine helped Jack with his English Literature classes?

_____

9. What has Christine just brewed?

_____

See Teacher's Manual

A: Do you work?

B: Yes, I work.

A: Where do you work?

B: I work in a printing company.

A: Who(m) do you work with in the printing company?

B: I usually work alone.

A: Have you been busy lately?

B: Yes, I have been very busy lately.

Do you study?

A: Yes, I do.

B: What do you study?

A: I study English.

B: Where do you study English?

A: I study English at Zoni Language Centers.

B: What have you studied recently at Zoni?

A: I've studied the Present Perfect recently.

Formation: **Regular Verbs**

$$\left\{ \begin{array}{c} \text{present tense of} \\ \textbf{have} \end{array} \right\} + \left\{ \begin{array}{c} \text{past participle} \\ \textbf{verb} \end{array} \right\}$$

Personal Pronoun	**have** (Contraction)	Past Participle
I	**have** (I've)	work**ed**
You	**have** (You've)	stud**ied**
He	**has** (He's)	paint**ed**
She	**has** (She's)	danc**ed**
It	**has** (It's)	rain**ed**
We	**have** (We've)	liv**ed**
You	**have** (You've)	clean**ed**
They	**have** (They've)	decid**ed**

Formation: Irregular Verbs

$$\left\{ \begin{array}{c} \textbf{present tense of} \\ \textbf{have} \end{array} \right\} + \left\{ \begin{array}{c} \textbf{past participle*} \\ \textbf{verb} \end{array} \right\}$$

Personal Pronoun	have	(Contraction)	Past Participle
I	**have**	(I've)	**begun**
You	**have**	(You've)	**come**
He	**has**	(He's)	**driven**
She	**has**	(She's)	**eaten**
It	**has**	(It's)	**fallen**
We	**have**	(We've)	**grown**
You	**have**	(You've)	**lost**
They	**have**	(They've)	**met**

*Note: See the irregular verb list in the Appendix for the base and simple past forms of these past participles as well as other irregular verb forms.

Lesson 4

THE PRESENT PERFECT
AND
THE PRESENT PERFECT
PROGRESSIVE

THE PRESENT PERFECT PROGRESSIVE

With a partner, ask and answer 5 questions about each other using the present perfect progressive with <u>since</u> or <u>for</u> in your answers. Then switch roles.

See Teacher's Manual

Examples

A: *How long have you been living in the United States?*

B: *I have been living in the United States since last year.*

A: *How long have you been studying English at Zoni?*

B: *I've been studying English at Zoni for 3 months.*

1. A: How long _____

   B: _____

2. A: _____

   B: _____

for	-Used with the present perfect progressive to express an
since	action that began in the past and continues into the present.

Examples
(Listen and repeat)

1 __I've__ **been** shopp**ing** **since** 9 o'clock.

2 __You've__ **been** liv**ing** in New York **for** 10 years.

3 __He's__ **been** study**ing** Karate **since** he was 20 years old.

4 __She's__ **been** paint**ing** watercolors **for** 15 years.

5 <u>**It's**</u> **been** rain**ing** for 3 hours.

6 <u>**We've**</u> **been** stand**ing** at attention **since** last night.

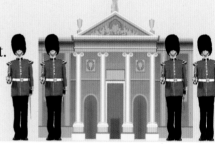

7 <u>**You've**</u> **been** surf**ing** the Net for 2 hours.

8 <u>**They've**</u> **been** gett**ing** along with each other for over fifty years.

Pair Practice

Since	- To indicate **when an action began**
For	- To indicate **the duration of an action**

Examples

I've been studying English at Zoni **since last summer**.

Natasha and Ilhan have been studying English at Zoni *for* **6 months**.

With a partner, fill in the blanks using the appropriate word, <u>since</u> or <u>for</u>.

1. It's been raining in northern California_____ yesterday.

2. Isabel has been studying here _____ 2 years.

3. Mr. Chen has been cleaning his car _____ two hours.

4. You and I have been living in New York_____ last winter.

5. Fernando has been working in the drugstore _____ three months.

6. Wilmer has been looking for a nice house_____ last June.

7. Fred and Wilma have been watching TV _____ almost 3 hours.

8. Liz has been staying with her daughter in Colombia_____ May.

9. Edna has been waiting for your call_____ several weeks.

10. Flor and Alejandro have been dancing the Tango _____they were teenagers.

Oral Practice
-Simple Present and Present Perfect Progressive

(Listen and repeat)

1

A: Do you work in that factory?

B: Yes, I work in that factory.

B: Yes, I do.

C: Who(m) do you work in that factory with?

B: I work with Martha.

C: How long have you been working in that factory?

B: I've been working in that factory since 1993.

2

A: Do you shop for groceries?

B: Yes, I shop for groceries.

B: Yes, I do.

C: Which supermarket do you shop at?

B: I shop at Save-Mart supermarket.

C: How long have you been shopping there?

B: I've been shopping there for a year.

130

Group Oral Interaction

In groups, practice the following combinations of question words using the verbs in parentheses. Follow the models on page 130.

(Teachers: Assess <u>Present Perfect Progressive</u> with <u>for</u> and <u>since</u> here.)

See Teacher's Manual

Who(m)...with How long...	Where How long...	Which How long...

1. A: Do _____? **(play/playing)**

B: Yes, _____.

B: Yes, _____.

C: Who(m) _____?

B: I _____.

C: How long _____?

B: I _____.

2. A: Do _____? **(study/studying)**

B: Yes, _____.

B: Yes, _____.

C: Where _____?

B: I _____.

C: How long _____?

B: I _____.

3. A: Do _____? **(dance/dancing)**

B: Yes, _____.

B: Yes, _____.

C: Which club _____?

B: I _____.

C: How long _____?

B: I _____.

Let's Review - Present Perfect and Count Nouns

> **more** _ _ _ _ _ _ _ _ _ _ **than**
< **fewer** _ _ _ _ _ _ _ _ _ _ **than**

= **as many** _ _ _ _ _ _ _ _ _ _ **as**
× **not as many** _ _ _ _ _ _ _ _ _ _ **as**

+ **the most** _ _ _ _ _ _ _ _ _ _
− **the fewest** _ _ _ _ _ _ _ _ _ _

(Elicit from the students)
(Listen and repeat)

1

Sam   *Erika*

Who **has eaten more** *apples*: Erika or Sam?

Erika **has eaten more** *apples* **than** Sam.

2

Jack   *Fernando*

Who **has bought fewer** *CDs*: Jack or Fernando?

Jack _____ .

ZONI ENGLISH SYSTEM ©   133

3

8 hours
8 hours

Who **has slept more** *hours*: your mother or your father?

My mother _____.

4

Amparo

Khalid

Who **has not met as many** *people* at the party **as** Amparo?

Khalid _____.

5

Who **has read the most** *books*?

_____.

Who **has read the fewest** *books*?

_____.

Katy   *Isabel*   *Mr. Hill*

6

Who **has run the most** *miles*?

_____.

Who **has run the fewest** *miles*?

_____.

Rebecca   10 miles   20 miles   9 miles
Carlos   *Paula*

134

Let's Review - Present Perfect and Noncount Nouns

>	**more** _ _ _ _ _ _ _ _ _ _	**than**
<	**less** _ _ _ _ _ _ _ _ _ _	**than**
=	**as much** _ _ _ _ _ _ _ _ _ _	**as**
×	**not as much** _ _ _ _ _ _ _ _ _	**as**
+	**the most** _ _ _ _ _ _ _ _ _	
−	**the least** _ _ _ _ _ _ _ _ _	

(Elicit from the students)
(Listen and repeat)

1

Rose
(12 min.)

Diana
(7 min.)

Who **has spent more** *time on the phone*: Rose or Diana?

Rose_____.

Diana_____.

2

Who **has made more** *money*: the lawyer or the bookkeeper?

The lawyer_____.

Doctor ($120,000)

The bookkeeper_____.

Who **has made more** *money*: the bookkeeper or the secretary?

The bookkeeper_____.

Bookkeeper ($24,000)

Who **has made the most** *money*?

The doctor_____.

Lawyer ($100,000)

Who **has made the least** *money*?

The bookkeeper and the secretary_____.

Secretary ($24,000)

Pair Practice

With a partner, ask and answer the questions below. Then switch roles.

1. Who has drunk more water: Peter or Lisa?

_____

2. Who has drunk less water: Katie or Lisa?

_____

3. Who has drunk as many bottles of water as Peter?

_____

4. Who hasn't drunk as much water as Katie?

_____

5. Who has drunk the most water?

_____

6. Who has drunk the fewest bottles of water?

_____

136   ZONI ENGLISH SYSTEM ©

Present Perfect = specific time not mentioned

- The emphasis is on an action that has occurred, not on when it occurred.
- Use "have" or "has" for short answers.

(Listen and repeat)

1. Have you met the new student?

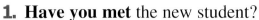

Yes...

Yes, I have.

No...

No, I haven't.

2. Has Patricia written a letter to her friend?

Yes, she has.

No, she hasn't.

3. Have they finished the project?

Yes, they have.

No, they haven't.

Group Oral Interaction

In groups, ask one another questions in a three-way conversation using the information below. Answer with affirmative or negative short answers as appropriate.

Example:

A: Have you bought any new CDs?
B: Yes, I have.
A: Has he bought any new CDs?
C: Yes, he has.

Base Verb	Information
buy	any new CDs
drink	beer
clean	your room
borrow	any money
lend	any money
see	a baseball game
read	any good novels
watch	TV in English
visit	the Statue of Liberty
make	new friends at Zoni
think	about your future
be	to Europe

ZONI ENGLISH SYSTEM ©

Pair Practice

Ask three original questions. Answer in affirmative or negative short answers. Then switch roles.

(Teachers: Assess Present Perfect with short answers here.)

Student A   *Have you?*   **Student B**

1. Have you eaten Sushi?   No, I haven't.

2. Have you seen the Atlantic Ocean?   Yes, I have.

3. _____?   No, _____.

Student B   *Have you?*   **Student A**

1. *Have you flown in a jet?*   *Yes, I have.*

2. _____   _____

3. _____   _____

Present Perfect vs. Simple Past

(Listen and repeat)

## Present Perfect	## Simple Past
no specific time mentioned	**specific time mentioned**
Examples	**Examples**
Have you played any tennis lately?	Did you play tennis last Saturday?
Yes, I have.	Yes, I did.
Has your cousin Rita called you recently?	Did your cousin Rita call you yesterday?
No, she hasn't.	No, she didn't.
Have you finished your homework yet?	Did you finish your homework at 4:00?
Yes, I have.	Yes, I did.
Has your brother taken a shower?	Did your brother take a shower at 9:30?
No, he hasn't.	No, he didn't.
Have John and Cindy seen any action movies lately?	Did John and Cindy see any action movies last weekend?
Yes, they have.	Yes, they did.

Oral Practice

Use the simple past tense with "when" or "what time" to indicate a specific time.
(Elicit from the students)
(Listen and repeat)

1. Have you been to the movies lately?

Yes, I've been to the movies lately.

Yes, I have.
When did you go?
I went last Tuesday and again last Saturday.

2. Have you eaten lunch yet?

Yes, _____.

Yes, _____.
What time _____?
_____ at 12:30.

3. Have you finished washing the dishes?

Yes, _____.

Yes, _____.
When _____?
_____ five minutes ago.

4. Have you put the turkey in the oven?

Yes, _____.

Yes, _____.
What time _____?
_____ at 5:15.

Pair Practice

Exercise I

With a partner, practice the dialogue based on the information in the box below.
Switch roles and repeat.

Example:

Student A

Student B

Student A: Have you <u>gotten a massage</u> (**1**) recently?

Student B: Yes, I have.

Student A: When did you <u>get</u> (**2**) the massage?

Student B: I <u>got</u> (**3**) the massage <u>yesterday</u> (**4**).

	1	**2**	**3**	**4**
Ex:	gotten a massage	get	got	yesterday
1.	flown to Florida	fly	flew	last Sunday
2.	bought food	buy	bought	2 days ago
3.	written to your friend	write	wrote	last week
4.	eaten fish	eat	ate	last night

Now, complete the blank boxes with your own information and
practice questions and answers with your partner based on your
information. Follow the example on page 142.

(Teachers; Assess Present Perfect vs. Simple Past here.)

See
Teacher's
Manual

1. _ridden on a bus_ ___ride___ 3. _____ 4. _____

A: _____

B: _____

A: _____

B: _____

2. _visited your country_ ___visit___ 3. _____ 4. _____

A: _____

B: _____

A: _____

B: _____

3. _swum in the ocean_ ___swim___ 3. _____ 4. _____

A: _____

B: _____

A: _____

B: _____

4. *seen a concert*   *see*   _____   _____

A: _____

B: _____

A: _____

B: _____

5. *rented a movie*   *rent*   _____   _____

A: _____

B: _____

A: _____

B: _____

6. _____   _____   _____   _____

A: _____

B: _____

A: _____

B: _____

Homework

Write questions and answers based on the information below. Use the present perfect or the simple past tense.

Examples:

[Karl / go to the gym / last week]

Did Karl go to the gym last week?

No, he didn't go to the gym last week.

[you / take / the TOEFL / yet]

Have you taken the TOEFL yet?

No, I haven't taken it yet.

1. [you / pay your rent / yet]

_____?

Yes, _____.

2. [Mr. and Mrs. Johnson / take a vacation / two years ago]

_____?

Yes, _____.

3. [Monica / read the newspaper]

_____?

No, _____.

4. [they / buy a bus pass]

_____?

No, _____.

5. [Lim-Soek / visit the doctor / yesterday]

_____?

Yes, _____.

6. [you / finish your homework]

_____?

Yes, _____.

146

Present Perfect
- an action that has already occurred
- a repeated action

Ex.

Didier *has learned* how to speak three languages.

Present Perfect Progressive
an action that began in the past and continues into the present

Ex.

Lisa *has been studying* French since last year.

(Listen and repeat)

Use the present perfect with repeated actions ("how many?"/"how often?").

How many times *have* Keith and Mickey *seen The Matrix*?
They *have seen* it 4 times!

Use the present perfect progressive for duration of an action ("how long?").

How long *have* Angélica and Rafaela *been waiting* on line for tickets?
They*'ve been waiting* on line for 2 hours!

Group Oral Interaction

See Teacher's Manual

In groups, create questions with "how many"/"how often" or "how long" and the present perfect or present perfect progressive tense and then provide answers. *(Teachers; Assess Present Perfect vs. Present Perfect Progressive here.)*

1. How long / you / study English?

_____

2. How many times / you / be to Madrid?

_____

3. How often / John / work out this month?

_____

4. How many languages / Wendy and Andrea / learn?

_____

5. How long / Janice / wait for her mother?

_____

6. How often / phone / ring in the last hour?

_____

7. How many countries / you / visit in your life?

_____

8. How long / Petra and Ivan / live in the U.S.?

_____

9. How often / rain / this summer?

_____

10. How many friends / you / make at Zoni?

_____

148

Homework

Use the present prefect or present perfect progressive as appropriate.

1. It _____ (**rain**) every day this week.

2. It _____ (**rain**) since this morning.

3. That cell phone _____ (**ring**) 3 times in an hour! It keeps distracting me.

4. The fire alarm _____ (**ring**) for 2 minutes, but no one has called the fire department yet.

5. Sofia _____ (**visit**) her mother since last Saturday.

6. Yoko _____ (**visit**) China several times in her life.

7. Mr. Johnson _____ (**teach**) English at Zoni for 3 years.

8. René _____ (**teach**) French at the college every summer.

9. John and Jimmy _____ (**lose**) every game so far.

10. Elio and Vanessa _____ (**not lose**) since the game started.

Dictation 4

(Listen to the teacher and write.)

1. _____

2. _____

3. _____

4. _____

5. _____

6. _____

7. _____

Bonus

Sing Along With Me

Have You Ever Been to Spain?

Pair Practice

See Teacher's Manual

A: Have you ever been to Spain?

B: No, I've never been to Spain.

A: Have you ever been to Mexico?

B: No, I haven't, but I'd like to go.

A & B: Why don't we go together?

A: Have you ever been to Spain?

B: No, I've never been to Spain.

A: Have you ever been to Ecuador?

B: Yes, I've been there many times before.

A: When was the first time?

B: I can't remember.

Have you ever been to _____?

Would you like to go there?

Act It Out

Practice in groups of 3 in order to "act it out" in front of the class. Choose countries to fill in the blanks.

 See Teacher's Manual

Anne: Good afternoon. How may I help you?

Lee: My brother and I want to go on a special vacation to someplace new and exciting.

Anne: Great. I can help you. What part of the world have you been thinking about?

Phil: We have been thinking about _____.

Anne: OK. Have you ever been to _____?

Lee: Yes, we've been there several times.

Anne: Have you ever been to _____?

Lee: Yes. I am from _____. We've been there many times.

Anne: Have you ever gone to _____?

Phil: No, we've never gone there.

Anne: Would you like to go to _____?

Lee: Sounds great.

Phil: Yeah, let's do it!

AMAZING KOREA

152

A Postcard to a Friend Back Home

Miki is from Tokyo, Japan. She and her brother are tourists visiting New York. Below is a postcard that Miki wrote to her friend, Takashi, in Tokyo.

Dear Takashi,

   I've only been in New York for 2 weeks, but I've already seen several interesting sights. I've been to Rockefeller Center, and I've also visited the Statue of Liberty. I haven't gone to Radio City Music Hall yet, but my brother and I are going to go there tomorrow. Yesterday, we saw Chinatown.
   Have you ever visited New York? If you haven't, you really should come here. It's a great city. I'll see you when I get home next month. I miss you.

   Love, Miki

Takashi Suzuki

Sakae Bldg. 37,
LL-111 Nishishinjuku, Shinjuku-ku
Tokyo 163-8001 Japan

Homework

Imagine that you are a tourist in New York. Write a postcard to a friend in your country describing the places you've visited. Use the sample postcard on page 153 as a guide. Include as many examples of the present perfect tense as you can.

A New and Exciting Vacation

Mr. and Mrs. Hart live in the United States. Mr. Hart has just retired from his job as an executive for a bank in downtown San Diego, California. Mrs. Hart has been retired from her job as a high school teacher for one year. Because both of the Harts now have a lot of free time, they want to plan a special vacation. They want to go somewhere new and exciting—a place where they've never been before. The problem is that they don't know where. The Harts are at the Bon Voyage travel agency, speaking to Ms. Smith, a travel agent.

Ms. Smith: Good afternoon, I'm Cecilia Smith. How may I help you, today?

Mr. Hart: Hello, Ms. Smith. I'm Joe Hart, and this is my wife, Paula.

Ms. Smith: Very nice to meet you, Mr. Hart, and you, too, Mrs. Hart.

Mrs. Hart: Please call me Paula.

Mr. Hart: And I'm Joe.

Ms. Smith: OK. And please call me Cecilia. Now, what can I do for you this afternoon?

Mrs. Hart: Well, Joe has just retired, and I've been retired since last year. We've done a lot of traveling in the past, but this year we want to take a special vacation to celebrate Joe's retirement. We'd like to go someplace where we've never been before.

Ms. Smith:	That sounds wonderful! I'm sure I can help you. Tell me, what part of the world have you been thinking about?
Mr. Hart:	We've been thinking about Europe since Joe decided to retire.
Ms. Smith:	Have you ever traveled to Europe before?
Mr. Hart:	Yes, we've been there several times, but we haven't been there for many years.
Ms. Smith:	Have you ever visited France? You haven't lived until you've seen Paris in the summer.
Mrs. Hart:	Yes, we know. We visited Paris in July of 1985.
Ms. Smith:	How about Italy or Germany?
Mrs. Hart:	We've been to Italy twice and Germany once, but I don't recall exactly when.
Ms. Smith:	Have you ever gone to London? It's one of our most popular tourist destinations.
Mrs. Hart:	Yes, we went to London in August of 1990. We saw Big Ben and the Changing of the Guard at Buckingham Palace. It was fabulous. That was the last time we were in Europe.
Ms. Smith:	Well, have you ever been to Spain?

Mr. Hart: No, as a matter of fact, we've never been to Spain. We made plans to go there in 1980, but we had to cancel them because I was too busy at work.

Ms. Smith: So then, would you like to go to Spain for your special vacation this year?

Mr. Hart: Yes, that sounds wonderful to me. What do you think, Paula?

Mrs. Hart: Spain sounds perfect!

Ms. Smith: OK. Currently, there are two great packages to choose from. The first one is a 3-week tour package that includes Madrid, Barcelona and Valencia. The second one is a 4-week tour package that includes Madrid, Barcelona, Valencia and a week in Palma de Majorca. Which package would you rather take?

Mrs. Hart: Oh, I'd rather take the second package. I've always wanted to see the city of Palma. What do you think, Joe?

Mr. Hart: Yes, I prefer the second package, too. I've heard that Palma is a marvelous city.

Ms. Smith: Wonderful. Would you excuse me for just one minute while I get all the information for you?

Mrs. Hart: Of course. Thank you very much.

Formation: Irregular Verbs

$$\left\{ \begin{array}{c} \textbf{present tense of} \\ \textbf{have} \end{array} \right\} + \left\{ \begin{array}{c} \textbf{past participle*} \\ \textbf{verb} \end{array} \right\}$$

Personal Pronoun	have	(Contraction)	Past Participle
I	**have**	(I've)	**begun**
You	**have**	(You've)	**come**
He	**has**	(He's)	**driven**
She	**has**	(She's)	**eaten**
It	**has**	(It's)	**fallen**
We	**have**	(We've)	**grown**
You	**have**	(You've)	**lost**
They	**have**	(They've)	**met**

*Note: See the irregular verb list in the Appendix for the base and simple past forms of these past participles as well as other irregular verb forms.

Lesson 5
MODALS

MODALS

can / could / be able to

**With a partner, tell each other things you <u>could</u>/<u>were able to</u>
("used to be able to") do in the past, but that you <u>can't</u>/<u>are not
able to</u> do now.**

See Teacher's Manual

Pair Practice

Examples

A: When I was a child, I could run very fast, but now I can't.

B: When I was 5 years old, I was able to speak some German, but now I'm not able to.

ZONI ENGLISH SYSTEM ©

Pair Practice

Student A makes a question using _can_ based on the statement provided.
Student B answers Student A's question using _be able to_.

Examples

Katy and Humberto **can** fix the TV.	Shoshana **cannot** speak French.
A: Can Katy and Humberto fix the TV?	**A: Can** Shoshana speak French?
B: Yes, they **are able to** fix the TV.	**B:** No, Shoshana **is not able to** speak French.

1. Victor and Mr. Coltrane **can** enjoy their vacations now.

A: _____

B: _____

2. I **cannot** see without glasses.

A: _____

B: _____

3. My wife **can** cook delicious seafood dishes.

A: _____

B: _____

4. Angelica **can** sense danger when she drives.

A: _____

B: _____

5. Robert's children **cannot** speak more than one language.

A: _____

B: _____

6. True love **can** pass the test of time.

A: _____

B: _____

7. My wife and I **can** have everything we desire if we are persistent.

A: _____

B: _____

Affirmative

[be able to - (specific past occurrence)]

Example

There was a big fire last night, but the
firefighters **were able to** put it out.

(Elicit from the students)
(Listen and repeat)

1. We went on vacation last summer.

We _____ visit England, France and Spain.

2. The final exam was a piece of cake.

I _____ finish it in 30 minutes.

3.

I _____ call my mother before the battery in my cell phone
went dead yesterday.

Bla Bla
Bla...

164

Negative

[not be able to - (specific past occurrence)
could not]

Example

There was a big fire last night, but, unfortunately, the firefighters
<u>couldn't</u>
<u>weren't able to</u> } put it out.

(Elicit from the students)
(Listen and repeat)

1. We went on vacation last summer.

We _____ } visit Italy because we didn't have enough time.
_____
skipped!!

2. The final exam was too hard.

I _____ } finish it in time.

"Time's up. Hand in your exams."

3. I _____ } call my father after the battery in my
_____ cell phone went dead yesterday.

Low battery
Good bye!

Pair Practice

With your partner, make sentences combining the action and time cues. Make one sentence with _could_ or _couldn't_ and another with _was able to/ were able to_ or _wasn't able to/weren't able to_.

Action		Time
Example:		
say the alphabet		she was in preschool

She **could** say the alphabet when she was in preschool.
She **was able to** say the alphabet when she was in preschool.

1. reach the table		he was a baby
2. speak correctly	 I don't want to get any bad grades.	she was in high school
3. play tennis		she lived in Paris
4. beat all competitors		he was the champion
5. practice his Spanish	 Hola, Cómo está?	he was very small

Group Oral Interaction

Using page 166 for cues, in groups, make sentences in the affirmative or negative using both <u>could</u> and <u>be able to</u>.

Example:

*She **could** say the alphabet when she was in preschool.*

*She **was able** to say the alphabet when she was in preschool.*

1. _____

   _____

2. _____

   _____

3. _____

   _____

4. _____

   _____

5. _____

   _____

Pair Practice

Tell your partner about what your family <u>could/couldn't</u> do or <u>were/weren't able to</u> do. Then switch roles.

*(Teachers: Assess **<u>can</u>**, **<u>could</u>** and **<u>be able to</u>** in the present and past, affirmative and negative here.)*

See Teacher's Manual

Pair Practice

Things my family members

<u>could</u> *or* **<u>were able to</u>** *do when they were young.*

Sister & Brother

Father & Mother

Grandfather & Grandmother

Homework

Answer using <u>could/couldn't</u> or <u>was/were able to</u>/ <u>wasn't/weren't able to</u>.

1. [can]

When I was in high school, I _____ play basketball because I was very tall.

2. [be able to]

I _____ speak when I was 6 months old.

3. [can]

When I lived in my country, I _____ walk to school because the school was very close to my house.

4. [be able to]

When I was a child, I _____ reach the table because I was too short.

5. [can]

I _____ recite the alphabet when I was in preschool,

but I _____ read.

6. **[be able to]**

I _____ eat a lot of food when I was young without gaining weight because I was very active.

7. **[can]**

When I was six years old, I _____ see very well, but by the time I was ten, I needed eyeglasses.

8. **[be able to]**

When I was a child, I _____ speak a little Italian, but I can't speak it now.

9. **[can]**

When I was in my country, I _____ talk to my cousins in person, but now we have to talk by phone.

10. **[be able to]**

I _____ understand my parents very well when I was a teenager.

ZONI ENGLISH SYSTEM ©

Things my family members
<u>could</u> *or* **<u>were able to</u>** *do.*

Make a sentence using either A (<u>could</u>) or B (<u>was able to</u>, <u>were able to</u>).

1. When I was 4 months old,

A: I _____

2. When Patricia was 1 year old,

B: she _____

3. When my brother was young,

B: he _____

4. When my brother and sister were in school,

A: they _____

5. While my parents were working,

B: we _____

Exercise II

Fill in the blanks with **was**/**were able to**, **wasn't**/**weren't able to** or **could**/
couldn't. If there is more than one correct answer, write both answers.

1. I _____ visit you last night because I didn't have time.

2. We _____ go to the concert last week because it was sold out.

3. Mike got up early last Saturday. That's why he_____ finish all
his work before 1:00 PM.

4. **a.)** When we went back to Venezuela last summer, we_____
visit all of our family because we didn't have enough time.

b.) However, we_____ visit our parents and grandparents.

5. Many people saw the two men rob the bank and gave the police a good

description. For that reason, the police _____ catch them quickly.

6. When I went to the supermarket on Saturday, I_____ buy some
delicious fruit, so I now I can make a fruit salad.

7. The firefighters _____ put out the fire quickly because it was
only a small fire.

8. I_____ call you yesterday because my phone wasn't working.

Affirmative

Use... **may** + **base verb**
might + **base verb**] to express possibility.

(Listen and repeat)

1
What are you going to do right now?
I'm not sure. I <u>may **go**</u> home or I <u>**might go**</u> shopping.

2
Are you going to go to the beach tomorrow?
I don't know. I <u>**might have to work**</u> tomorrow.

3
Who is the girl with Robert?
I'm not sure. She <u>**might be**</u> his sister, or she <u>may **be**</u> his girlfriend.

4
Do you think you <u>**might go**</u> to Kevin's party next Saturday?
I <u>may **go**</u>, but it depends on what time I finish work.

5
I don't understand the homework. Who(m) can I call for help?
I can't help you, but Gary <u>**might be able to help**</u>. He's so smart.

6
Do you want to go to the disco tonight after class?
I'm really tired. I think I <u>may **go**</u> to bed early tonight.

Complete the Conversation
Group Oral Interaction

See Teacher's Manual

In groups, fill in the blanks with <u>may</u> or <u>might</u>. Then perform the dialogue with each person in the group playing one of the roles.
*(Teachers: Assess **may** and **might** here.)*

Patricia: I'm having a barbecue at my house next Saturday. Would you like to come?

Keith: I'd love to, but I'm not sure I can because I_____ have to work next Saturday.

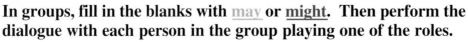

Patricia: You _____ be able to ask one of your coworkers to work for you.

Keith: That's a possibility. I_____ ask Rick because he owes me a favor. In fact, I'll try to call him right now.
(Keith calls on his cell phone, but there's no answer.)

Well, he's not home. He_____ still be at work.
(Keith calls at work, and Rick answers.)

Rick: Yes, I think I can work for you next Saturday. There's only one little problem. My in-laws _____ be coming to visit. To be honest, I'd rather work than visit with them, but my wife will be mad if I work during their visit.

Keith: When will you know for sure if they're coming or not?

Rick: I _____ know tonight, but I'll know for sure by tomorrow night. I'll let you know as soon as I can.

Keith: Thanks a lot.

Rick: No problem.

Could - Polite Request

Could you...?

Case # 1: Use **"could you"** + **base verb** in a question when you want <u>another person</u> to perform an action.

(Elicit from the students)
(Listen and repeat)

1
Excuse me. **Could you** please tell me the time?

Sure. It's 10:35.

2
Excuse me, teacher. **Could you** repeat the answer, please?

Of course. I said the past of "buy" is "bought."

3
Excuse me, sir. _____ please take off your hat? I can't see the movie.

Sure. Sorry about that.

4
Excuse me, driver. _____ tell me when we get to Fifth Avenue, please?

Yes, of course. It's about one mile from here.

5
Carla, _____ please lend me $5.00 until tomorrow?

Sure. Here you are.

6
Waiter, _____?

_____?

_____. _____.

_____.

Could I ...?

Case # 2: Use **"could I" + base verb** in a question when <u>you</u> want to perform an action.

(Elicit from the students)
(Listen and repeat)

1
Excuse me. **Could I** sit here?

Sure. The seat isn't taken.

2
Excuse me, teacher. **Could I** go to the bathroom?

Of course. Go ahead.

3
_____ please turn on the TV?

Certainly.

4
Excuse me, sir. _____ get change for a dollar, please?

OK. Here are 4 quarters.

5
Karl, _____ borrow $5.00 until tomorrow?

Sure. Here you are.

6
Excuse me waiter, _____?

_____.

Group Oral Interaction

In groups, come up with examples using "<u>Could you...?</u>" and "<u>Could I...?</u>" in the classroom.

Example:

Mr. Jones, **<u>could you</u>** help us with the present perfect tense?

<u>Could I</u> ask you a question about "polite requests?"

1. Could you _____ ?

2. _____ ?

3. _____ ?

4. Could I _____ ?

5. _____ ?

6. _____ ?

Homework
Which modal is correct?

[
will   **should**
might   **can**
couldn't   **must**
]

1. [Advice]

Isabel _____ go on a diet.

2. [Obligation]

I _____ study for the exam.

3. [Ability]

Mr. Walensa _____ speak English.

4. [Possibility]

When are you going to visit your family?

I _____ visit them next month.

5. [Promise]

The president says he _____ help poor people.

6. [Past Ability (negative)]

I ran out of time, so I _____ finish my test.

Let's + base verb

Why don't we...?
Why don't you...?
Why don't I...?

Affirmative Responses

(Listen and repeat)

1

Let's dance!

OK. I'd like to.

2

Why don't I call you a cab?

Thank you.

3

Let's not tell anyone about this.

Sure, I can keep a secret.

4

Why don't we get Chinese food tonight?

That sounds good to me.

5

Let's go to the movies this weekend.

Great idea! I'll go.

Negative Responses (Listen and repeat)

1
Why don't we fly first class?

No. We can't afford to.

2
Let's go to the gym to work out.

No thanks. I'm too tired today.

3
Let's go over the homework again.

No, it's not necessary. I understand it now.

4
Why don't we go to the park today?

I think it will rain today. Let's go tomorrow, OK?

5
Why don't you turn off the air conditioning?

I'd rather not turn it off. I prefer it on.

Note: "**Shall I...?**" and "**Shall we...?**" are also used to make suggestions, but the use of "shall" is more formal and less commonly used in conversation.

Shall I inform you when the guests have arrived, Madam?

Yes, please do.

ZONI ENGLISH SYSTEM ©

Group Oral Interaction

See Teacher's Manual

Jack is having trouble understanding the present perfect and present perfect progressive, and he failed the last test. In your groups, come up with 5 suggestions for Jack to help him understand the tense and pass the next test. Use **"Let's,"** **"Why don't you…?"** and **"Why don't we…?"** One person in your group will read your suggestions for Jack to the class. *(Teachers: Assess suggestions here.)*

Example:

Why don't we study together for the next test?

1. _____

2. _____

3. _____

4. _____

5. _____

Homework

Make suggestions using the information below and verbs in parentheses.

1. Why don't I_____? **(help)**

Thank you very much.

2. Let's_____. **(review)**

No thanks. I think I understand the tense now.

3. Why don't we_____? **(listen to)**

Sure. What kind of music do you like?

4. Let's_____. **(watch)**

OK. I think there's a good movie on cable tonight.

5. Why don't you_____? **(study)**

I will study more for the next test, I promise.

6. Let's_____. **(go on vacation)**

Paris sounds wonderful! But can we really afford it?

Affirmative

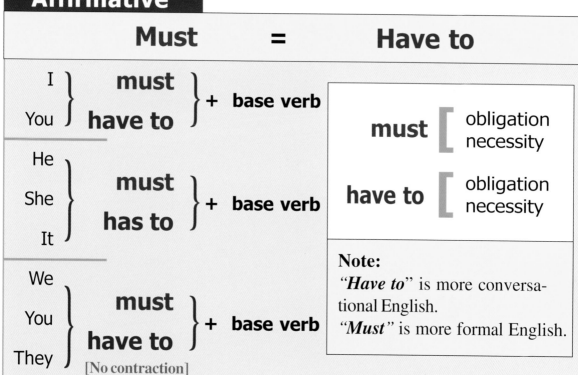

Must	=	Have to

I, You } must / have to } + base verb

He, She, It } must / has to } + base verb

We, You, They } must / have to } + base verb
[No contraction]

must [obligation / necessity

have to [obligation / necessity

Note:
"*Have to*" is more conversational English.
"*Must*" is more formal English.

Must (Listen and repeat)

People **must** drink more liquids when the weather is hot.

Students **must** come to class and participate in class if they want to learn English.

Cars **must** stop at a red light, slow down at a yellow light and go at a green light.

Have to (Listen and repeat)

Today is the first day of the month. I **have to** pay the rent.

Mindy **has to** go to bed early tonight because she **has to** get up early tomorrow.

Today is my sister's birthday. I **have to** get her a nice present.

Pair Practice

Ask your partner a question using *have to*. Your partner answers using *must*. (*Teachers: Assess **have to** and **must** here.*)

Example [Charlie / do to pass his test / study a lot]

*A: What does Charlie **have to** do to pass his test?*

*B: He **must** study a lot.*

1. [Jake / clean / his room]

A: _____

B: _____

2. [Students / do to learn English / practice a lot]

A: _____

B: _____

3. [Drivers / obey / the rules of the road]

A: _____

B: _____

4. [We / do to buy a house / save money]

A: _____

B: _____

5. [Jacqueline and Steven / pass / the college-entrance exams]

A: _____

B: _____

6. [You / do to be a success in the business world / speak English]

A: _____

B: _____

184

Homework
Use **must** or have to

To Take a Vacation

My father told us that if we want to go away on vacation this year, all the family

members _____ do their part. My brother _____ bring

home a good report card. That means my brother _____ study hard in

order to get all "A's." My sister_____ help my mother clean the house

and take care of our pets. That means she _____ feed them and take

them for a walk every day. I _____ improve my English. To do that,

I _____ read books in English and

also watch TV programs in English.

And, of course, my father _____

continue to work hard at his job in the factory

while my mother takes care of the house and of

my brother, my sister and me.

Negative

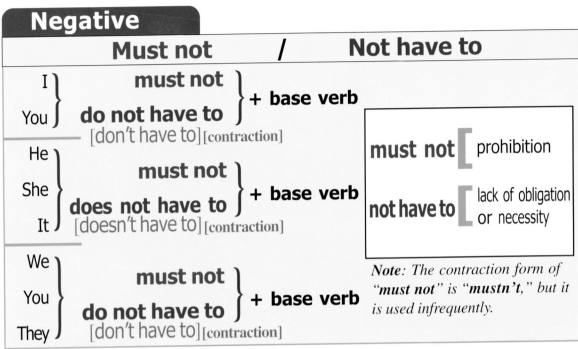

Must not	/	Not have to

I / You : **must not** / **do not have to** [don't have to] [contraction] + **base verb**

He / She / It : **must not** / **does not have to** [doesn't have to] [contraction] + **base verb**

We / You / They : **must not** / **do not have to** [don't have to] [contraction] + **base verb**

must not [prohibition

not have to [lack of obligation or necessity

Note: The contraction form of "must not" is "mustn't," but it is used infrequently.

Must not (Listen and repeat)	Not have to (Listen and repeat)
You **must not** smoke in the classroom.	I **don't have to** work today because it's the Fourth of July.
You **must not** drink alcohol and drive.	Mother says I **don't have to** eat *all* my vegetables, but I **have to** eat *some* of them.
You **must not** trespass on private property.	We **don't have to** take the umbrella today because it isn't raining.
You **must not** go when the light is red.	The teacher said we **have to** do page 15, but we **don't have to** do page 16. Page 16 is optional.
You **must not** sleep at work.	You **don't have to** buy me flowers every week. It's not necessary because I already know you love me.

186

Group Oral Interaction

In groups, fill in the blanks using <u>must not</u> or <u>don't/doesn't have to</u>.
*(Teachers: Assess **<u>must not</u>** and **<u>not have to</u>** here.)*

1. Alice _____ exercise because she is sick.

2. I _____ get up at 6:00 a.m. because my job starts at noon.

3. Husbands and wives _____ keep secrets from each other if they want to have a good marriage.

4. You _____ run so fast, or you'll trip and fall down.

5. He _____ pay $500 for a color TV. I'm sure he can find a cheaper one.

6. The doctor says that Lisa _____ eliminate sugar from her diet, but she does have to reduce the amount she consumes.

7. I _____ forget to do the homework.

8. You _____ drink alcohol and drive. It's dangerous and against the law.

9. David's parents_____ help him with his schoolwork because he's so smart.

10. You _____ say you love me because your actions show that you do.

11. We _____ enter that building. The sign says, "Keep Out!"

ZONI ENGLISH SYSTEM ©

187

Homework
Which modal is correct?

$$\left[\begin{array}{cc} \text{will} & \text{let's} \\ \text{may} & \text{could} \\ \text{must not} & \text{be going to} \end{array}\right]$$

1. [Ability- Past]

When he was young, my grandfather _____ walk very well, but now he needs a cane.

2. [Promise]

I promise that I _____ call you tomorrow.

3. [Suggestion]

It's a beautiful day!_____ go to Central Park.
Good idea!

4. [Possibility]

Why is the baby crying?

I'm not sure. She_____ be wet.

5. [Prohibition]

We _____ speak Spanish during our English class.

6. [Future Planning]

We _____ eat out tonight because we don't feel like cooking.

188

Dictation 5

(Listen to the teacher and write.)

1. _____

2. _____

3. _____

4. _____

5. _____

6. _____

7. _____

Group Work
Error Review

Each one of the sentences below contains one error. In groups, find and correct the error.

Example:

would

Manuel ~~wood~~ rather learn English than French.

1. New York has most people than Paris.

2. Paris has lesser traffic than London.

3. Juan has less dollars than Freddie.

4. Cristina has the least dollars.

5. Jane doesn't has as much money as Amy.

6. Jack moved to Florida on 1989.

7. Roger goes to the movies in weekends.

8. Zoni New Jersey is located in Bergenline Boulevard.

9. Paula goes to school every days.

ZONI ENGLISH SYSTEM ©

10. Enrique has class three time a week.

11. Manuela usually is 10 minutes late to class.

12. I am living in New York for 2 years.

13. Johnnie should speaks more English at work.

14. Have you saw any good movies lately?

15. Karen just has received some very good news.

16. Julieta has been studying English since 6 months.

17. How much times have you gone to Miami?

18. Harry must to see Peter right away.

19. When I was younger, I can run really fast.

20. Keith and Sandra wasn't able to go out last Saturday.

Homework
Going to a Concert

Wilson, Jose and Manuel are students at Zoni Language Centers in Queens. They all work during the day and study English in the evenings from 6:00 to 8:00 p.m. Wilson has just found out that there is going to be a concert at Madison Square Garden in Manhattan in two weeks. The concert is going to be on a Saturday night. It will feature various Latin Pop artists.

Wilson: Hey guys, there's going to be a great concert at Madison Square Garden two weeks from Saturday. The cheap seats are only $20. Let's go!

Manuel: Who's going to perform?

Wilson: Shakira, Christina Aguilera, Chayanne and lots of others.

Jose: That sounds great. I'd love to go, but I might have to work that weekend. I'm going to ask my boss if he needs me that Saturday night or not.

Manuel: I'd like to go, too, but I usually work on Saturday nights. I'll ask my boss if I can have that night off, but he'll probably say no. We've been really busy lately, and he needs everybody to work.

Wilson: Well, I need to buy the tickets before the concert gets sold out. Could you both find out as soon as possible and let me know?

Jose: Look, why don't you buy me a ticket now? I think I can go, but if not, I might be able to sell my ticket to somebody. My neighbor, Carlos, bought a ticket to a Shakira concert last year, but then he couldn't go because he got sick. Maybe he'll buy my ticket if I can't go.

Manuel: Don't buy a ticket for me yet. I'm going to ask my boss tonight, and I'll let you know tomorrow if I can go or not.

192

Wilson: Okay, I'll wait until tomorrow but no longer than that. If we wait too long, we probably won't be able to get seats. And I don't want to miss this concert.

Manuel: No problem. I promise that I'll call you tomorrow night.

Wilson: One more thing. Could you both give me the cash *before* I go for the tickets? I'm sorry but I don't have enough money to pay for all three tickets in advance.

Manuel: Sure, no problem. I'll pay you tomorrow night if my boss says I can have that night off.

Jose: I'll pay you right now because I definitely want a ticket. Here's a twenty-dollar bill.

Manuel: Thanks.

Jose: You're welcome.

Homework
Reading Comprehension

In complete sentences, answer the following questions based on the reading.

1. What has Wilson just found out?

_____

2. Where is the concert going to take place?

_____

3. Which artists are going to perform at the concert?

_____

4. How much are the cheap seats?

_____

5. Why does Manuel think he probably won't be able to have the night of the concert off?

_____

6. Who might buy Jose's ticket if he can't attend the concert?

_____

7. What happened to Carlos after he bought a ticket to a Shakira concert last year?

_____

8. Can Wilson afford to pay for all three tickets in advance?

_____

9. When is Manuel going to ask his boss if he can have the night of the concert off?

_____

10. What is Wilson afraid may happen if they wait too long to buy tickets?

_____

Group Oral Interaction

When we go to the next level, we…

In groups, talk about what you've learned in this course and what you would like to learn in the next course. Using your discussion, write a letter together to your future teacher in the next Zoni course you are going to take.

Dear Teacher,

CONGRATULATIONS!
Welcome to the next level.

Final Oral Exam

A: Hello. My name is Lili. What's your name?

B: My name is Jeremy. How are you today?

A: I'm fine, thanks. How about you?

B: I'm fine, too. Do you work?

A: Yes, I do.

B: **Where** do you work?

A: I work in a factory in Manhattan.

B: **How long have you worked** there?

A: I've worked there **for** 8 months. **Do you** play sports?

B: Yes, I do.

A: **What** do you play?

B: I play soccer.

A: **How long have you been playing** soccer?

B: I've **been playing** soccer **since** I was a child. Where are you from?

A: I'm from Ecuador.

B: **Do you visit** your country?

A: Yes, I do.

B: **How often do you** visit your country?

A: I visit my country **once a year**. I **usually** go back in July. **Do you** drink coffee?

B: Yes, I always drink coffee in the morning, but I never drink it at night. **What did you do** last weekend?

A: Last weekend I **went** to a birthday party. **Did you** buy any CD's last month?

B: No, I **couldn't** buy any because I didn't have any extra money. **Have you seen** the Statue of Liberty yet?

A: No, I haven't, but I plan to see it soon. **Have you ever** been to Europe?

B: No, I've **never** been there. Excuse me, what time is it?

A: It's 4:00.

B: Sorry, but I'm late for an appointment. I **have to** go. **It's been** nice **talking** to you.

A: **It's been** a pleasure for me, too. I **should** also go. **Why don't we** leave together?

B: OK, **let's** go!

Affirmative — Ability - Present Tense

can = be able to

Personal Pronoun	can base verb [No contraction]
I	
You	
He	
She	**can** run fast.
It	
We	
You	
They	

Personal Pronoun	Verb to be	[Contraction]	able to base verb
I	**am**	[I'm]	
You	**are**	[You're]	
He	**is**	[He's]	
She	**is**	[She's]	**able to** run fast.
It	**is**	[It's]	
We	**are**	[We're]	
You	**are**	[You're]	
They	**are**	[They're]	

Negative	Ability - Present Tense

cannot	=	not be able to

Personal Pronoun	cannot can't [Contraction]	base verb	Personal Pronoun	Verb to be	[Contraction form 1] [Contraction form 2*]	not able to *able to	base verb
I			I	am	[I'm] [-------]		
You			You	are	[You're] [You aren't*]		
He			He	is	[He's] [He isn't*]		
She	cannot	run fast.	She	is	[She's] [She isn't*]	not able to *able to	run fast.
It	can't		It	is	[It's] [It isn't*]		
We			We	are	[We're] [We aren't*]		
You			You	are	[You're] [You aren't*]		
They			They	are	[They're] [They aren't*]		

Affirmative   Ability - Past Tense: __used to be able to__

__could__   =   __be able to (past)__

Personal Pronoun	__could__ base verb [No contraction]	Personal Pronoun	__Verb__ (past) __to be__ [No contraction]	__able to__ base verb
I		I	__was__	
You		You	__were__	
He		He	__was__	
She	__could__ run fast years ago.	She	__was__	__able to__ run fast years ago.
It		It	__was__	
We		We	__were__	
You		You	__were__	
They		They	__were__	

Negative	Ability - Past Tense: **did not use to be able to**

Could not = Not be able to (past)

Personal Pronoun	could not / couldn't [Contraction]	base verb	Personal Pronoun	Verb to be [Contraction*]	not able to *able to	base verb
I			I	**was** [wasn't*]		
You			You	**were** [weren't*]		
He			He	**was** [wasn't*]		
She	**could not**	run fast years ago.	She	**was** [wasn't*]	**not able to**	run fast years ago.
It	**couldn't**		It	**was** [wasn't*]	***able to**	
We			We	**were** [weren't*]		
You			You	**were** [weren't*]		
They			They	**were** [weren't*]		

ZONI ENGLISH SYSTEM ©

REGULAR VERBS

Verb	Simple Past	Past Participle	Verb	Simple Past	Past Participle
answer	answered	answered	love	loved	loved
arrive	arrived	arrived	miss	missed	missed
ask	asked	asked	mix	mixed	mixed
borrow	borrowed	borrowed	need	needed	needed
call	called	called	open	opened	opened
carry	carried	carried	paint	painted	painted
clean	cleaned	cleaned	play	played	played
close	closed	closed	practice	practiced	practiced
cook	cooked	cooked	pray	prayed	prayed
cry	cried	cried	push	pushed	pushed
dance	danced	danced	rain	rained	rained
decide	decided	decided	rent	rented	rented
discuss	discussed	discussed	repeat	repeated	repeated
finish	finished	finished	rest	rested	rested
fix	fixed	fixed	start	started	started
hate	hated	hated	stop	stopped	stopped
help	helped	helped	study	studied	studied
hurry	hurried	hurried	visit	visited	visited
invite	invited	invited	walk	walked	walked
jump	jumped	jumped	want	wanted	wanted
kiss	kissed	kissed	wash	washed	washed
laugh	laughed	laughed	watch	watched	watched
like	like	liked	whistle	whistled	whistled
listen	listened	listened	wink	winked	winked
live	lived	lived	work	worked	worked
look	looked	looked			

IRREGULAR VERBS

Verb	Simple Past	Past Participle	Verb	Simple Past	Past Participle
become	became	become	leave	left	left
begin	began	begun	let	let	let
blow	blew	blown	lie	lay	lain
bring	brought	brought	lose	lost	lost
buy	bought	bought	make	made	made
catch	caught	caught	meet	met	met
come	came	come	read	read	read
cost	cost	cost	ride	rode	ridden
cut	cut	cut	run	ran	run
do	did	done	say	said	said
drink	drank	drunk	see	saw	seen
drive	drove	driven	sell	sold	sold
eat	ate	eaten	send	sent	sent
fall	fell	fallen	sing	sang	sung
feel	felt	felt	sit	sat	sat
fight	fought	fought	sleep	slept	slept
find	found	found	speak	spoke	spoken
fit	fit	fit	spend	spent	spent
fly	flew	flown	stand	stood	stood
forget	forgot	forgotten/forgot	swim	swam	swum
get	got	gotten/got	take	took	taken
get up	got up	gotten up	teach	taught	taught
give	gave	given	understand	understood	understood
go	went	gone	wake	woke	woken
grow	grew	grown	wear	wore	worn
have	had	had	win	won	won
know	knew	known	write	wrote	written